MW01446109

BOOK
NOOKs

Inspired Ideas for Cozy
Reading Corners and
Stylish Book Displays

BOOK NOOKs

Vanessa Dina + Claire Gilhuly

Photography by Antonis Achilleos

A special thanks to the following contributors
whose beautiful homes appear in this book:

Amber Hampton, Jim Kaylor, Jason Koxvold, Marios Lyssiotis,
Alessandra Mortola, Lydia Pursell, Mindi Shapiro,
Lauren Shaver, Hiro Sone, and Alistair Turnbull

Text copyright © 2024 by Chronicle Books LLC.
Photographs copyright © 2024 by **Antonis Achilleos**.

All rights reserved. No part of this book may be reproduced in any form without written permission from the publisher.

Library of Congress Cataloging-in-Publication Data available.

ISBN 978-1-7972-2587-6

Manufactured in China.

FSC — MIX Paper from responsible sources FSC™ C169962

Design by **Vanessa Dina**.
Typeset in Amarga and TT Commons Pro.

10 9 8 7 6 5 4 3 2 1

Chronicle books and gifts are available at special quantity discounts to corporations, professional associations, literacy programs, and other organizations. For details and discount information, please contact our premiums department at corporatesales@chroniclebooks.com or at 1-800-759-0190.

Chronicle Books LLC
680 Second Street
San Francisco, California 94107
www.chroniclebooks.com

SERRA
BETTINA RHEIMS
FEMALE TROUBLE
SCHIRMER ART BOOKS
Marcel Broodthaers
Draft No. 4

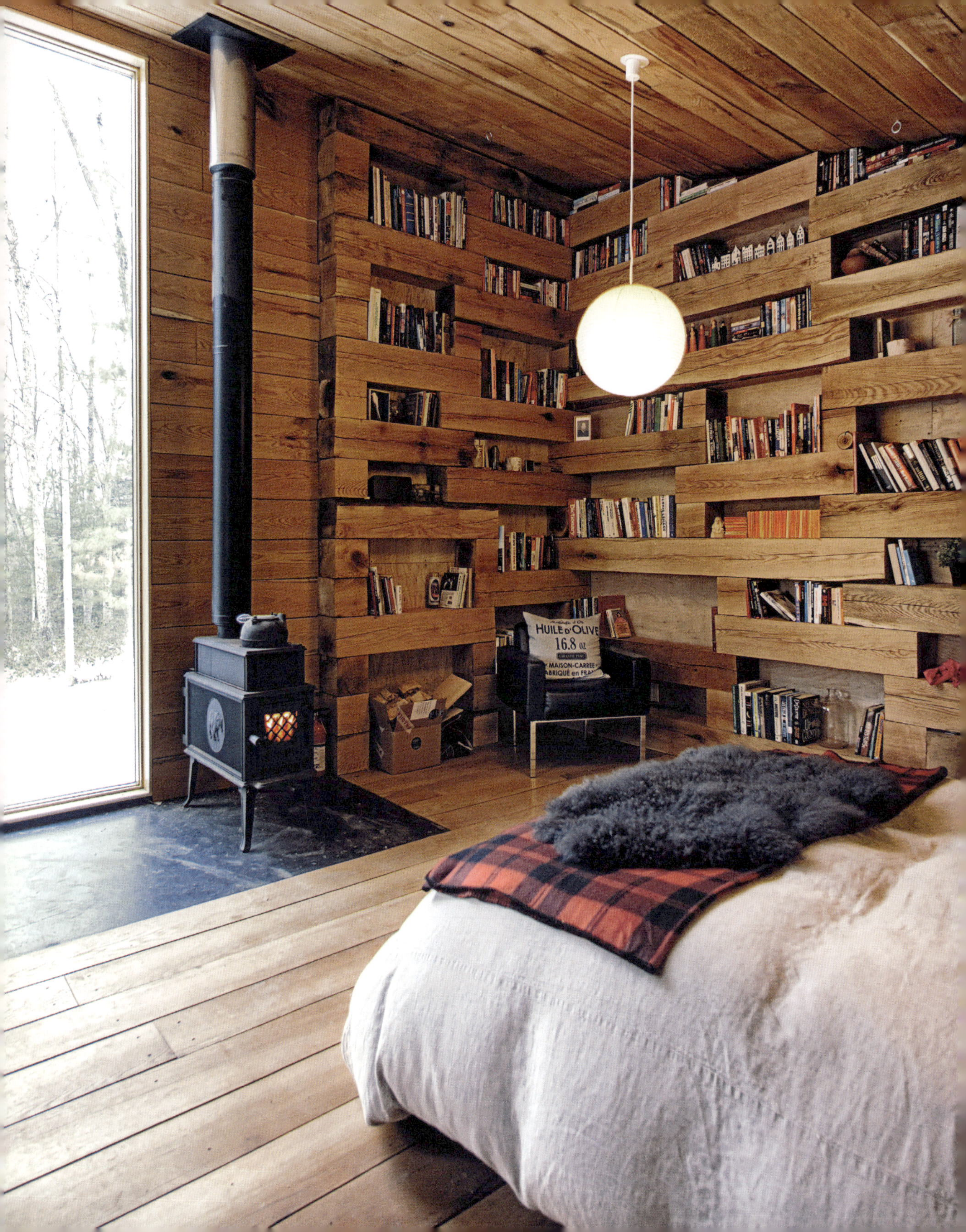
HUILE D'OLIVE
16.8 oz
MAISON-CARREE

INTRODUCTION 8

THE NOOKS

1 Classic 13
2 Small Space 23
3 Bedside 37
4 Bathroom 45
5 Baby 51
6 Kids 59
7 Cookbook 71
8 Bar 81
9 The Collector 91
10 The Gardener 99
11 The Artist 109
12 Colorful 119
13 Neutral 131

BOOKS BEYOND NOOKS 138

INTRODUCTION

As bookworms know, home is where the books are. As stylists know, books are an essential element of home décor. A home without books is less, well, homey and less stylish.

Whether you hope to organize a surplus of books, add some pizzazz to an existing room, or create a new, inviting nook that encourages reading, you've come to the right place. These pages brim with original ideas for styling gorgeous book displays and irresistible spots to read around the home.

Not only do books educate, inspire, and provide a welcome escape, but they are also beautiful objects. So much craft and consideration goes into the making of each and every volume. One hardcover represents the thoughts, opinions, and decisions of countless individuals. From the conception of an idea to the writing, editing, design, proofing, printing, and binding of a book, the process of bookmaking is a true labor of love.

The fact that books are thought-provoking *and* attractive makes them the ideal piece of functional décor for any room in a home. If you think of books as décor and treat them with integrity, it follows that you would want to display them in a beautiful way. Enter *Book Nooks*. By being thoughtful about how you organize and display books, style shelves, and design a space, you can create a nook that you'll want to read and spend time in, a nook that feels as good as it looks. This book will show you how.

Styling a book nook is an art, but it's one that can be imitated—and eventually learned—quite easily. Numerous factors will, of course, steer your design: which room the nook will live in, the amount of space you have, the style of your home, how the nook will be used (for reading, for décor, or for both purposes equally?), and so forth. For example, a baby book nook in a sweet nursery will require a wholly different design approach than a chic bar cart that hosts cocktail books. These spaces serve varying purposes and have distinctive aesthetics; the nooks within them should be designed accordingly.

DIANE ARBUS REVELATIONS
BELLOCQ
70s Style & Design
THE GEOMETRY OF PASTA
SNOWDON
DAVID BAILEY Locations
JEANLOUP SIEFF
MIKE & DOUG STARN
DAVID BAILEY BIRTH OF THE COOL
DAVID BAILEY ARCHIVE ONE

Paul McCartney
THE LYRICS
EDITED WITH AN INTRODUCTION BY PAUL MULDOON
Alexey Brodovitch
NOTES on DECOR etc.
PAUL FORTUNE
MARC HOM PROFILES
Interiors Atelier AM
VOGUE LIVING HOUSES, GARDENS, PEOPLE

Thankfully, this book is packed with innovative and unique ideas for book nooks of all shapes, sizes, and styles. Got a green thumb *and* an insatiable love of books? Discover ways to show off your books and plants together in the gardener nooks on pages 98 to 107. Working with limited space? Delight in the inventive ways to store and display books in small nooks on pages 22 to 35.

As a bonus, you'll find considered reading lists from celebrated contributors, including Gillian Flynn, Alex Elle, and PEN America. Food blogger and author Nik Sharma shares his best-loved cookbooks; *Cup of Jo's* Joanna Goddard points to her favorite memoirs; bestselling author Jasmine Guillory lists her go-to romance novels. These pages overflow with book recommendations across genres, as well as miscellaneous bookish content, from fun crafts to do with books to a list of gorgeous must-see libraries around the world.

Book Nooks is full of ideas for collecting, storing, displaying, and celebrating books, books, and more books! The hope is that you discover an abundance of inspiration in these pages and that, no matter how much space you have or what your aesthetic is, this styling guide helps you create the book nooks of your wildest bibliophile dreams.

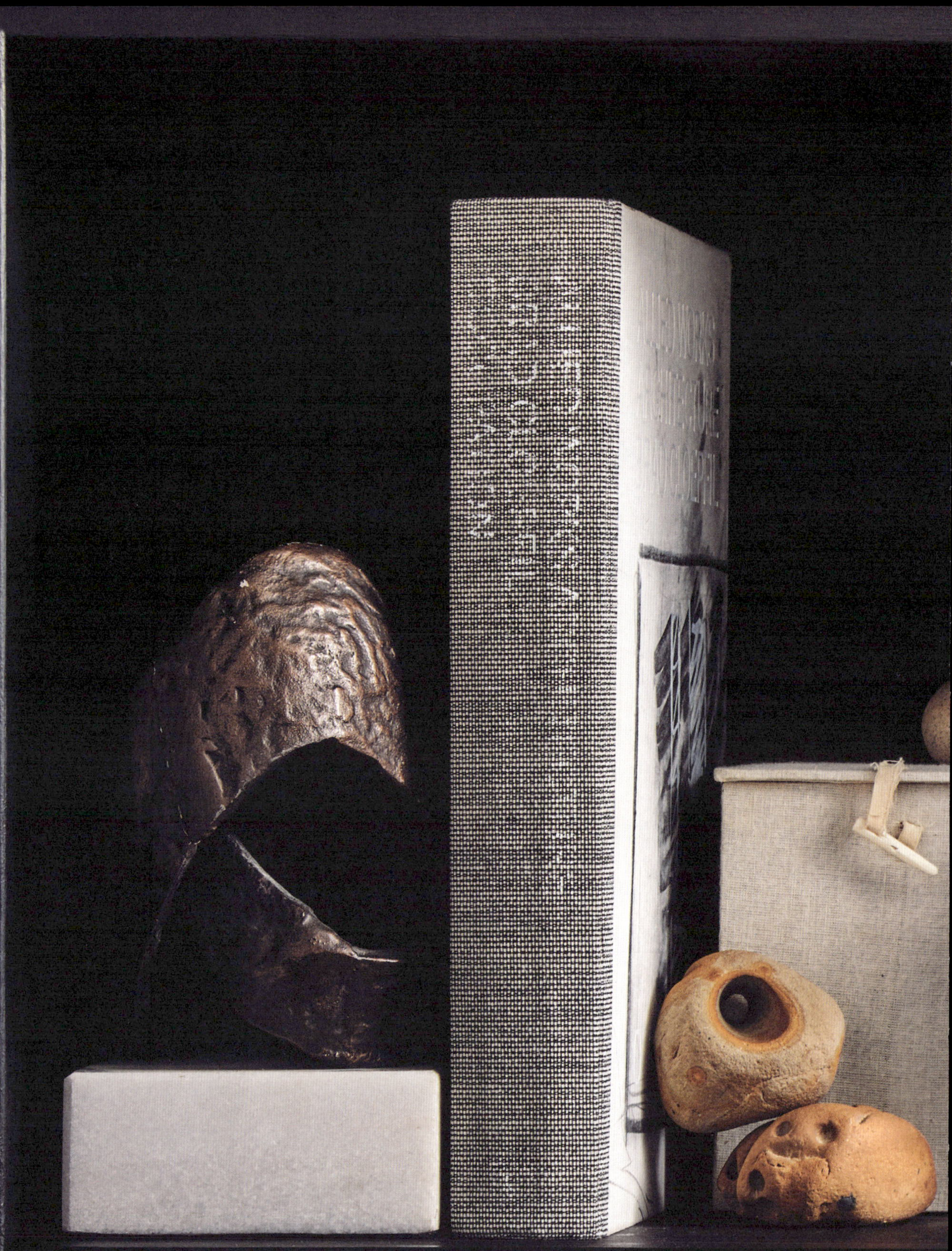

NOOK
1

CLASSIC

BEFORE THEY PASS AW
INTERIORS
BOUCHON
FARROW&BALL DECORATING with COLOUR

Classy and Classic

A crackling fire. Leather-bound books. Mahogany wood paneling. If this is what you picture when you think *book nook*, you're not alone. There's something deeply inviting about this traditionally styled space. It's classic for a reason.

Create a cozy feeling in your own home library by using timeless, naturally derived materials like leather, wood, and faux animal hides in warm, rich hues. Upholstered furniture, layered rugs, and piles of throw blankets add softness and a sense of luxury. Light a fire or a few candles, curl up with an Austen or a Brontë novel, and you'll be instantly transported to another time and place.

A shelf with a set of matching books is a handsome look and fitting for a traditional living room. It can be an investment to buy a brand-new set, so look for secondhand options at flea markets, thrift stores, or used bookstores.

Most likely, your space will suggest the best way to organize your library: alphabetically by title, the author's first name, or the author's last name; by genre; by color; or by size. In a traditional book nook like this one, organize the shelves using a tried-and-true method, such as alphabetization. In a colorful nook, you might opt to categorize books by hue for a rainbow effect. In a kid's book nook, you could sort books by topic—and so forth.

Books as Objects

Books with object appeal—like the leopard-spotted volume on page 14—can act as décor pieces on your coffee or end table. Stack two or three coffee table books in a color palette that complements your overall space for an effortless look.

Beautifully designed coffee table books not only make a design statement, but they also act as markers of taste and identity. Are you a travel enthusiast? Announce your favorite destination with a book from Assouline's travel series, whether on Tulum, Cairo, or the Amalfi Coast. Art aficionado? Celebrate your favorite artists with oversize monographs. These pieces will reveal your interests in a subtle way—plus, they're fun to flip through on a rainy day.

Leave books open to a favorite page—book interiors are meant to be seen and admired! And since an open book occupies about the same amount of space as two books side by side, this is an excellent way to take up more real estate on a coffee table. When opened to a full spread of photographs or illustrations, the book itself becomes a piece of art. (Try it with this book opened to the spread on pages 120 and 121!)

KELLY WEARSTLER DOMICILIUM DECORATUS
NEAR & FAR
Equestrian Life from Riding Houses to Country Estates
INTERIOR TRANSFORMATIONS
PERFECT ENGLISH TOWNHOUSE
INTERIORS
LONDON CALLING
BACON, FREUD, KOSSOFF, ANDREWS, AUERBACH, AND KITAJ
A TIME TO CELEBRATE FARMER
THOMAS O'BRIEN LIBRARY HOUSE
AN ADVENTUROUS LIFE
GLOBAL INTERIORS BY TOM STRINGER
ATLAS OF THE CIVIL WAR
FLORES-VIANNA HAUTE BOHEMIANS
THE ALLURE OF HORSES ASSOULINE

A PLACE TO CALL HOME
ARRIVING HOME
RICHARD GILLETTE
NICKY HASLAM
AND DREAMS OF HOME

A Functional Book Stack

A tall stack of books acts as an end table in this cozy reading nook. This is the perfect use for a surplus of oversize books—coffee table books, art books, even cookbooks. Opt for large, heavy books, keeping the biggest on the bottom. Books of similar size work best, as you want enough surface area on top to host a coaster and a mug of tea, or a glass of whiskey for evening reading.

Book stacks can also function to create dimension on a bookshelf or an end table. Use them to elevate a framed photo or clock, or layer them underneath a lamp to add height as needed. Featuring items on different levels is more pleasing to the eye than keeping everything uniform and on one flat plane.

Stack books from largest to smallest on a side table or stool for an attractive effect. At the end of a traditional English writing desk, this aged wooden stool holds a set of classic leather-bound books, complementing the library at the far end of the room (as seen on page 14).

GILLIAN FLYNN'S Favorite Mysteries

"The mystery genre, I truly believe, contains some of the most vivid characters, brilliant plots, and clever social commentary around. And while I love a good traditional mystery (I discovered Agatha Christie at the age of twelve and never looked back), I also adore the hard-boiled attitude of noir, the cold-water shock of thrillers, and the delicious unease of the gothic. Here are my ten favorites."

Kate Atkinson, *Case Histories*

Agatha Christie, *And Then There Were None*

Wilkie Collins, *The Woman in White*

Daphne du Maurier, *Don't Look Now*

Thomas Harris, *Red Dragon*

Patricia Highsmith, *The Talented Mr. Ripley*

Shirley Jackson, *We Have Always Lived in the Castle*

Dennis Lehane, *Mystic River*

Ross Macdonald, *The Drowning Pool*

Ellen Raskin, *The Westing Game*

GILLIAN FLYNN is the *New York Times* bestselling author of *Gone Girl*, *Dark Places*, and *Sharp Objects*. She lives in Chicago with her husband and children.

NOOK
2

SMALL SPACE

rEAd

Small Nooks Are Made for Books

Small spaces that might otherwise go unused or feel awkward—like a nonworking fireplace, an alcove under the stairs, or a cupboard without a door—make excellent book nooks. Fill them with books and they instantly become eye-catching and surprising décor moments.

When decorating a small space with books, get creative with organization and orientation. Try stacking books with their pages, rather than their spines, facing outward, as in this fireplace. (Of course, this should be done only with books that won't need to be accessed or used frequently, since hiding their spines makes it difficult to locate a particular title.) Arrange them vertically and horizontally in groups of six or seven to create a checkerboard effect. Or, lean the books diagonally in alternating rows—sloping to the right, then left, then right—for a zigzag effect (see page 26). The neutral color of the pages ensures this kind of pattern play is subtle and chic.

If you have books with dyed edges, play with different arrangements that highlight those beautiful blocks of pages. (Paint book blocks yourself or color them with markers for a fun craft project!) Feel free to be creative, and enjoy the process of designing your little library.

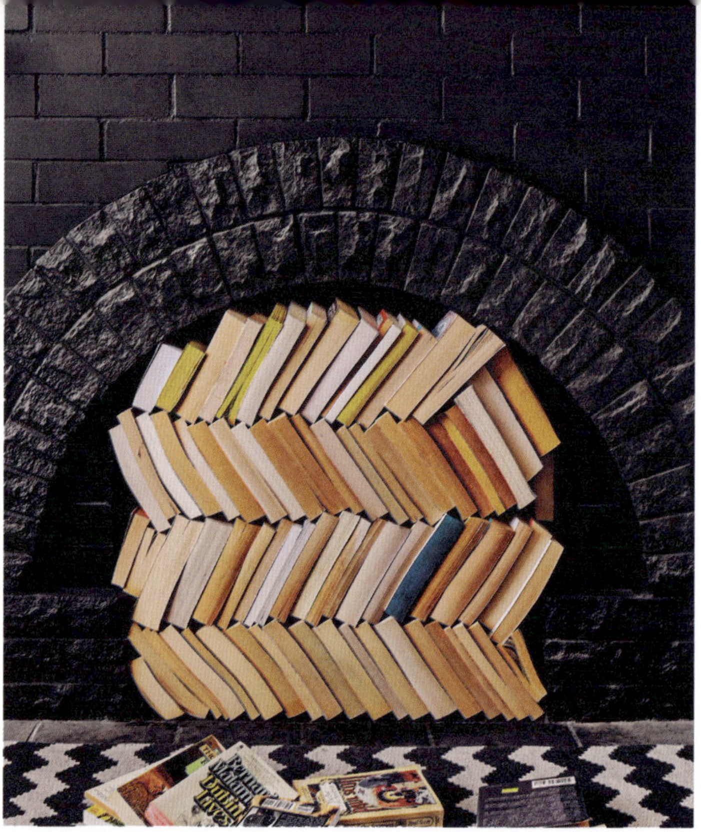

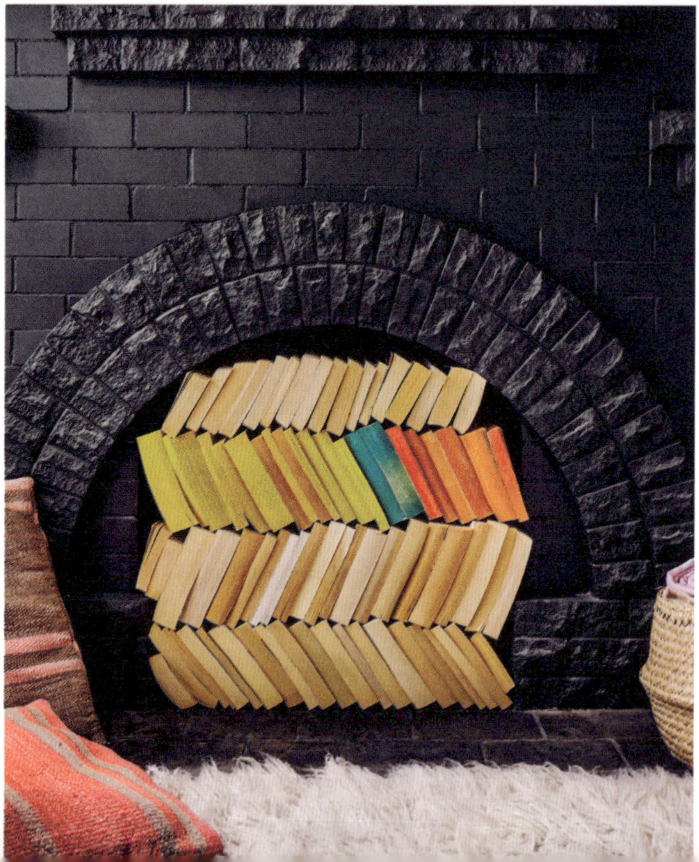

JOANNA GODDARD'S Favorite Memoirs

"Sometimes I imagine people walking down a street in New York City. If you're a toddler, you notice the dogs and gate latches. If you're a teenager, you see only teenagers. If you're a graphic designer, the typography of street signs. An arborist, the trees. A driver, the potholes. The same world looks very different to different people. I've always been curious to know what it's like to be someone else, and luckily, memoirs deliver just that. For example, Tara Westover writes about growing up in a survivalist family in Idaho; Andre Agassi describes winning eight Grand Slam tennis championships; Chrysta Bilton explains how she discovers she has more than thirty-five siblings; and Paul Kalanithi shares what it's like to realize you're dying—and soon. Here are those memoirs, plus more favorites."

Andre Agassi, *Open*

Chrysta Bilton, *Normal Family*

Amy Bloom, *In Love*

Tina Fey, *Bossypants*

Jayson Greene, *Once More We Saw Stars*

Paul Kalanithi, *When Breath Becomes Air*

Chanel Miller, *Know My Name*

Marjane Satrapi, *Persepolis*

Connie Wang, *Oh My Mother!*

Tara Westover, *Educated*

JOANNA GODDARD runs *Cup of Jo*, the popular women's lifestyle site, which covers style, culture, food, relationships, and parenting. She has a new weekly newsletter called *Big Salad*, and her writing has also appeared in *Glamour*, *Elle*, the *New York Times*, and *New York Magazine*. She lives with her two chatty children in Brooklyn, and you can follow her on Instagram at @cupofjo.

CHERRY BOMBE
CHERRY BOMBE
BOMBE
CREATIVE SPACES
Meggs
A History of Graphic Design
VAN NOSTRAND REINHOLD
THE END OF PRINT: THE GRAPHIC DESIGN OF DAVID CARSON LEWIS BLACKWELL
carson: 2nd sight BLACKWELL
The Family Meal
The Art of VOGUE Photographic Covers
HISTORY OF ART BY H.W. JANSON
FORAGED FLORA
THE CHASE BY THE CHASE How a graphic design consultancy thinks it thinks
TERRA INCOG
Pentagram

If you're short on space, books can stand in for furniture—as an end table between chairs, as a side table at the end of a couch, as a bedside table, or even as a coffee table if you place two stacks side by side. This hack is particularly useful in a small home and creates a one-of-a-kind mini book nook. If the book stack is a semipermanent fixture, place a small bud vase atop it with a single bloom for a sweet décor moment.

Have some tired old books lying around? Wrap them in pretty paper to create a matching set that is pleasing to the eye. Find luxe paper at any craft or stationery store, or cover them in simple construction paper in your favorite color to complement the room's décor. Black paper mirrors the wallpaper in this vignette, though pastel pink, white, or green paper would be lovely here as well.

HOTEL CHIC AT HOME
IN WITH THE OLD

ARCHITECTURE OF THE AMERICAN SOUTH
BON VOYAGE

ARRIVING HOME
A Thousand Days of Magic
Willem de Kooning
AXEL VERVOORDT
The Jewellery of Roman Britain
The Gardens of Luciano Giubbilei

PROVENCE THE ART OF LIVING
A TIME TO CELEBRATE
LONDON CALLING
BACON, FREUD, KOSSOFF, ANDREWS, AUERBACH, AND KITAJ
INTERIORS
INTERIOR TRANSFORMATIONS
PERFECT ENGLISH TOWNHOUSE

Color Matching

Displaying books in the same color palette as their surroundings creates a striking effect. Decorative books get nestled onto a staircase in this stylish home, but only those with a blue, black, or white cover! To match the black staircase and blue tiger-patterned wallpaper in this small nook, these homeowners thoughtfully limited the color palette in their book stack. The result is a cohesive and sophisticated décor statement in an unexpected place. As guests venture upstairs, they're delighted by these casually placed piles of books, and the dark colors allow the pieces of dried coral to really pop.

To re-create this in your own home, display books in colors that match the environment. In a neutral room, for example, choose books with cream, tan, or stone-colored covers. Take this approach to the next level by displaying books that match not only the color scheme but also the theme of your space. For example, in a beach house with blue wallpaper, display books related to the sea in all different hues of blue and white.

Small and Surprising

A fireplace and a staircase might not be typical places to keep books, but both can work beautifully if done right. If you have a surplus of books that you want to hold on to and are worthy of display, consider other lieus around the home that could host a petite and potentially surprising book nook: perhaps on a windowsill, on a mantel, or above a doorway. Architectural quirks, particularly in older buildings, often provide the trappings for a tiny library that will surprise and delight. And in small homes and apartments, maximizing storage space is key. Here, books are stashed beneath a bench—a clever space-saving hack that adds a pop of décor in an unusual place.

MINA STONE
COOKING FOR ARTISTS
My Paris Kitchen
Nigel Slater
Season

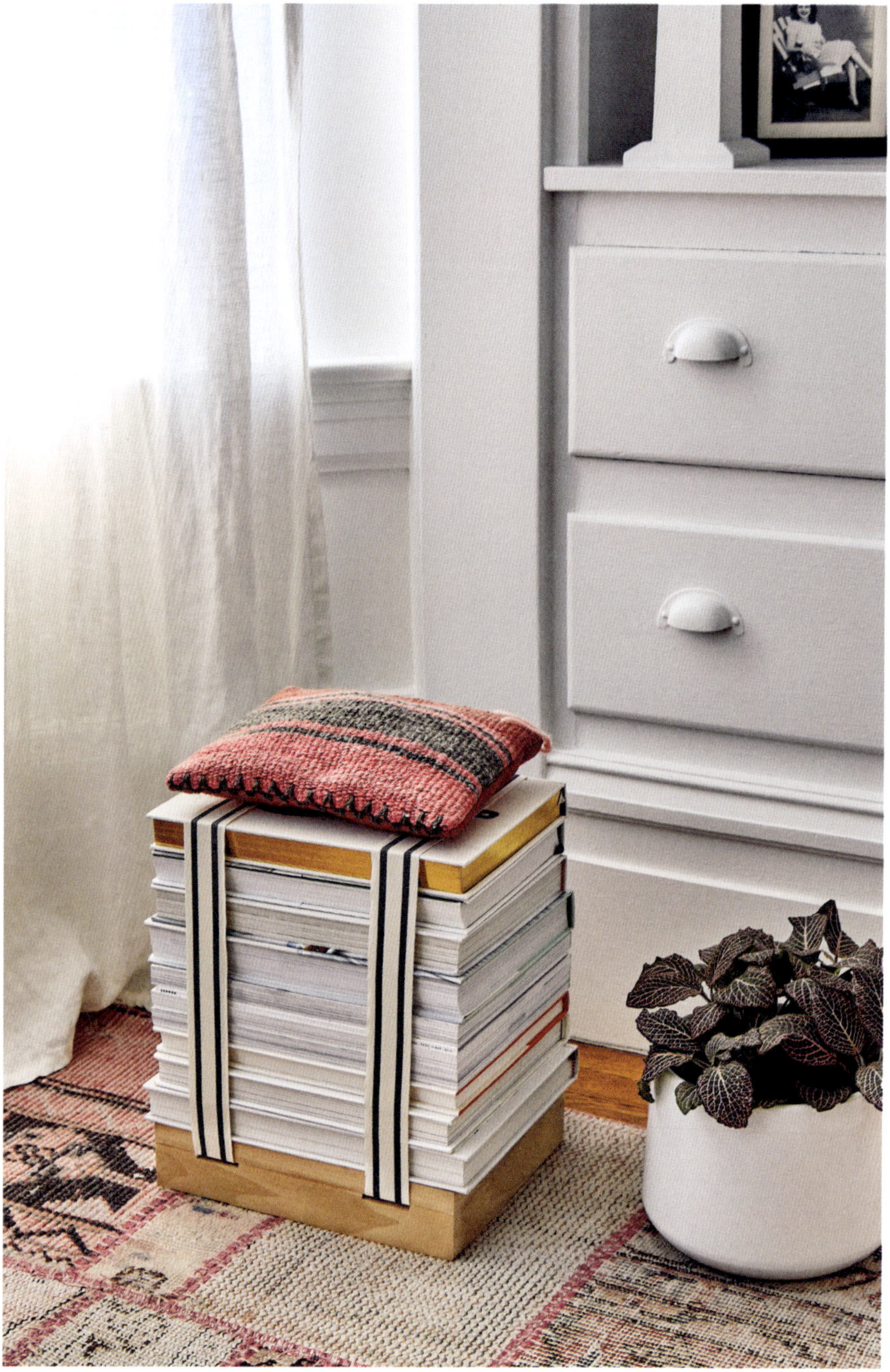

Book Crafts

Rather than donating old books to your local library or second-hand bookstore (which is always a fantastic option!), consider using them for craft projects. Here, large books of similar size are stacked on a block of wood and secured with thick straps to fashion a small stool. With a petite, comfortable cushion: Voilà! It becomes a darling spot to perch. Not only does this create more seating in your small nook, but it's also a unique book storage solution and a custom décor piece.

Get creative with other book crafts: Sketch line art on book pages and frame them to create a gallery wall. Make bookmarks out of old book spines. Convert a book into a keepsake box by hollowing out the inside, then place it on a shelf or coffee table or give it to a child so they can stash their treasures. Make rosettes out of book pages for an everlasting flower arrangement. Possibilities abound!

Reckitt
THE ART OF FEMINISM
CHRONICLE BOOKS
BLEGVAD
THE PINK BOOK
CHRONICLE BOOKS
SUNSET SEEKING
CHRONICLE BOOKS

BEDSIDE

NOOK
3

SELF-CARE IN UNDERWEAR
THE DHARMA BUMS Jack Kerouac
AFTER the RAIN
JUNG Dreams
ONE HUNDRED YEARS OF SOLITUDE
Lorrie Moore Bark
ASTROLOGY LOVE & SEX
THE FIRST BAD MAN A NOVEL BY MIRANDA JULY

A Sacred Space for Self-Care

Getting into bed after a long day should feel like an act of self-care. To create a soothing space for rest and relaxation, fill your bedside book nook with beloved books that bring you joy, as well as accessories that add beauty and peace: a bud vase of pretty flowers, an attractive journal with your favorite pen, a scented candle, an eye mask, or calming crystals. Souvenirs from your travels or framed photos fill a book nook with happy memories, while cozy items such as fluffy slippers, a terry cloth robe, a soft throw blanket, and pillows make your bedside extra inviting.

Keep petite and favorite books nearby, particularly those that are easy to dip in and out of, like collections of short stories or poetry. Reading for just ten minutes before bed can mentally prepare you for slumber, and waking with a poem can set your day on the right track. The stories of Jhumpa Lahiri and Alice Munro or the poems of Mary Oliver and Pablo Neruda are welcome salves from daily stressors.

To create a space that invites romance and encourages connection with your partner(s) (or yourself!), stash romance novels and nonfiction books about sex on your bedside table or bedside bookshelves.

Here, soft shades of pink—in the stool, carpet, sheets, and vase—act as a throughline, making this space feel cohesive and extra feminine.

Your bedroom should be a space for self-care, whether that means a calming room for journaling, rest, and sleep and/or an inviting space for romance, intimacy, and connection. Skip the TV and design a book nook that supports your sleep and your sex life—two healthful pursuits!

ALEX ELLE'S Most Trusted Books on Healing and Self-Love

"Reading has played an enormous role in my self-healing journey. These books have been trusted companions that I turn to again and again for teachings on love, mindfulness, grief, forgiveness, and self-knowledge, supporting my growth and empowering my work as a matriarch of healing."

Tabitha Brown, *Feeding the Soul*

Thema Bryant, PhD, *Homecoming*

Yasmine Cheyenne, *The Sugar Jar*

Pema Chödrön, *When Things Fall Apart*

Camille Dungy, *Soil*

Thích Nhất Hạnh, *The Art of Living*

bell hooks, *All About Love*

Kristi Nelson, *Wake Up Grateful*

Nedra Glover Tawwab, *Drama Free*

Michelle Zauner, *Crying in H Mart*

ALEXANDRA ELLE is a restorative writing teacher, the host of the *hey, girl* podcast, and the author of the *New York Times* bestselling *How We Heal*, as well as *After the Rain*, *In Courage Journal*, and several more books and journals. She leads workshops, online courses, and retreats to help people find their voices and power through writing, breathwork, and self-care practices. She lives outside of Washington, DC, with her husband and three daughters.

These gorgeous built-in bookshelves demonstrate another way to store and display books in a bedroom. Not only are built-ins a useful solution for book storage, but they can also be an attractive décor element and act as a makeshift headboard. Style your built-ins or floating shelves with art, framed photos, plants, and tchotchkes to add personality to your space.

JASMINE GUILLORY'S Must-Have Romance Novels

"I love reading romance for the same reason I love writing romance: It makes me think about people in a holistic way, about their personalities and families and wants and needs, and the ending makes me satisfied. I hesitate to call this list a best-of list; my feelings on *best* and *favorite* change from week to week and year to year and mood to mood. But this is a list of ten romance novels that I loved completely, that I always want to push into anyone's hands when they tell me they're looking for a new book to read."

Sarah Adler, *Mrs. Nash's Ashes*

Beverly Jenkins, *Destiny's Embrace*

Leah Johnson, *You Should See Me in a Crown*

Christina Lauren, *The Unhoneymooners*

Sangu Mandanna, *The Very Secret Society of Irregular Witches*

Alexa Martin, *Intercepted*

Alisha Rai, *Partners in Crime*

Farrah Rochon, *The Boyfriend Project*

Amy Spalding, *For Her Consideration*

Tia Williams, *Seven Days in June*

JASMINE GUILLORY is a *New York Times* bestselling author. Her novels include *The Wedding Date*, the Reese's Book Club selection *The Proposal*, and *Drunk on Love*. Her work has appeared in the *Wall Street Journal*, *Cosmopolitan*, *Bon Appétit*, and *Time*, and she is a frequent book contributor on the *Today Show*. She lives in Oakland, California.

NOOK
4

BATH ROOM

HERRIOTT GRACE
SPEAK ITALIAN
KAFKA · THE JUDGEMENT and IN THE PENAL COLONY
THE ALAN CLARK DIARIES · THATCHERS FALL · PHOENIX
MARX · THE COMMUNIST MANIFESTO · PHOENIX
TOBIAS WOLFF · Two Boys and a Girl
T. CORAGHESSAN BOYLE · She Wasn't Soft
WILL SELF · A Story for Europe
Gerard Manley Hopkins
As kingfishers catch fire
THE DHARMA BUMS Jack Kerouac

Dip In, Dip Out, Get Out

Having something to read while bathing or otherwise spending stretches of time, ahem, in the loo is welcome. As with a bedside book nook, lighter, dip-in-dip-out books make excellent bathroom reading material. Guests can flip to a page at random and learn something or be inspired in less than five minutes. No need here for long-winded novels or scholarly tomes, which most people won't have time for.

Collections of famous quotes, roundups of historical figures, profiles of empowered women, and the like are much better bathroom offerings when compared with denser reading. Be wary of magazines, which become dated and irrelevant quickly. The exceptions to this rule are well-designed zines or vintage magazines, both of which make a stylish statement.

Entertain guests with humorous bathroom books, if that's your style. These can be on the nose or otherwise comical.

To class up your powder room, opt for petite art-driven books. Shelve bathroom books on the windowsill, on the back of the toilet, or on a small stool or table, depending on how much space you have. Choose diminutive books that won't take up too much room, and coordinate the colors of your book stack with your bathroom accessories. In this powder room, a dominant and classic palette of black and white sets the stage, while pops of red—in the wall print, the peony, a few books, and even the tube of lipstick—add fun color and create a cohesive look.

Ayesha
Curry
Ayesha Curry I know this to be true
Jacinda Ardern I know this to be true
René Redzepi I know this to be true
CHRONICLE BOOKS
There Are Girls like Lions
RODIN

Even the bathroom can benefit from books! Who doesn't like to admire beautiful illustrations, read a lovely poem, or laugh at a joke while passing the time?

Merberg/
Bober
PAINTING WITH
PICASSO
KUIPERS/TOLEDANO
POLLY DIAMOND
2
chronicle books
Stutzman/
Fleck
TINY T. REX
and the Perfect Valentine
Alkayat
Cosford
FRIDA KAHLO
Ekstrand
Swaddle Me Up

NOOK
5

BABY

Library for a Budding Bookworm

Surround your newborn with books from the moment they come home from the hospital. Having books on display and easily accessible will instill a love of reading from an early age. Ignite their imagination, stoke their love of learning, share stories to expand their horizons, and open doors to other worlds and ways of thinking. The realm of reading has so much to offer young minds, and nurturing this skill can never start too soon.

When designing your baby's nursery, think about how and where books might be featured. It's easy to create a baby book nook no matter how much space you have. Babies are little, so baby book nooks can be small as well.

By thinking outside the box, you'll realize how many opportunities abound for book nooks, even in a tiny nursery: Floating shelves and small ledges attached to walls offer places to store and showcase books. Over-the-door storage, such as a hanging rack, allows for a stash of books to sit on the back of a door or inside a closet, out of sight. Reimagine a kitchen cart as a mini library—or use a wagon! Pile books on a window seat. Fashion a trio of bins for easy dumping, labeling each bin with the desired item ("books," "stuffed animals," or "toys"). All of these solutions are simple, effective, and require hardly any room. Book storage in a nursery should be easy to use and accessible, but it should also let you keep books out of view. As a busy parent, you'll want to quickly stash books without worrying about them looking neat.

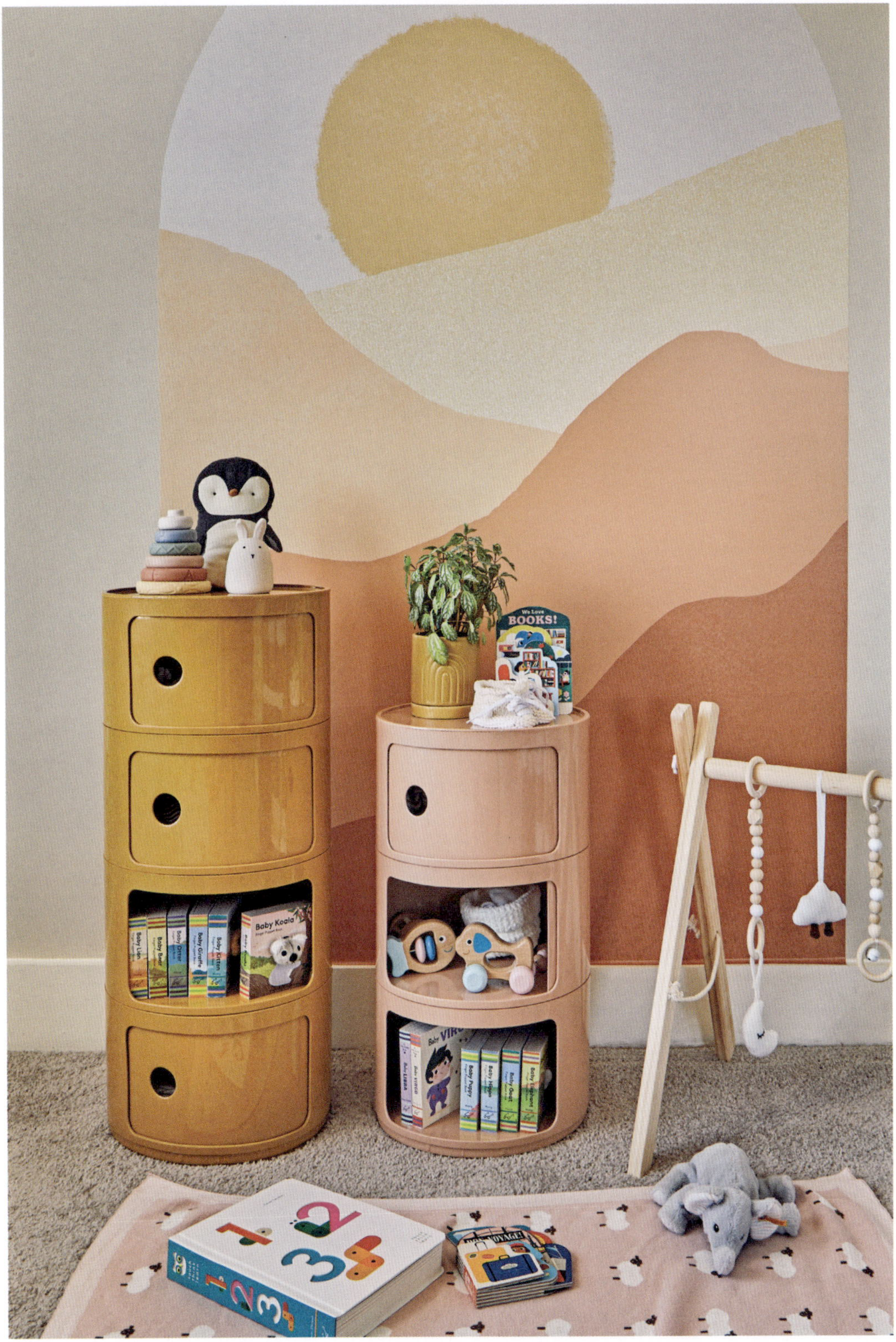
We Love
BOOKS!
Baby Koala

In a themed nursery, display books on the same topic. An under-the-sea nursery, for example, might house the *Baby Fish*, *Baby Octopus*, and *Baby Narwhal* board books in the finger puppet series, along with *The Rainbow Fish* by Marcus Pfister and other underwater-themed books. A turtle mobile above the crib, a whale stuffed toy, and a blue area rug would round out this theme perfectly.

A comfy chair—preferably one that rocks—is essential in a nursery. Creating a cozy nook that fits you and your child will help establish a regular reading routine.

Look for cute cabinets to hide the mess in a nursery. These sweet stackable units have closed compartments, which allow busy parents to stuff them with odds and ends for quick cleanup, as well as open cubbies that show off favorite books and toys and keep them in arm's reach.

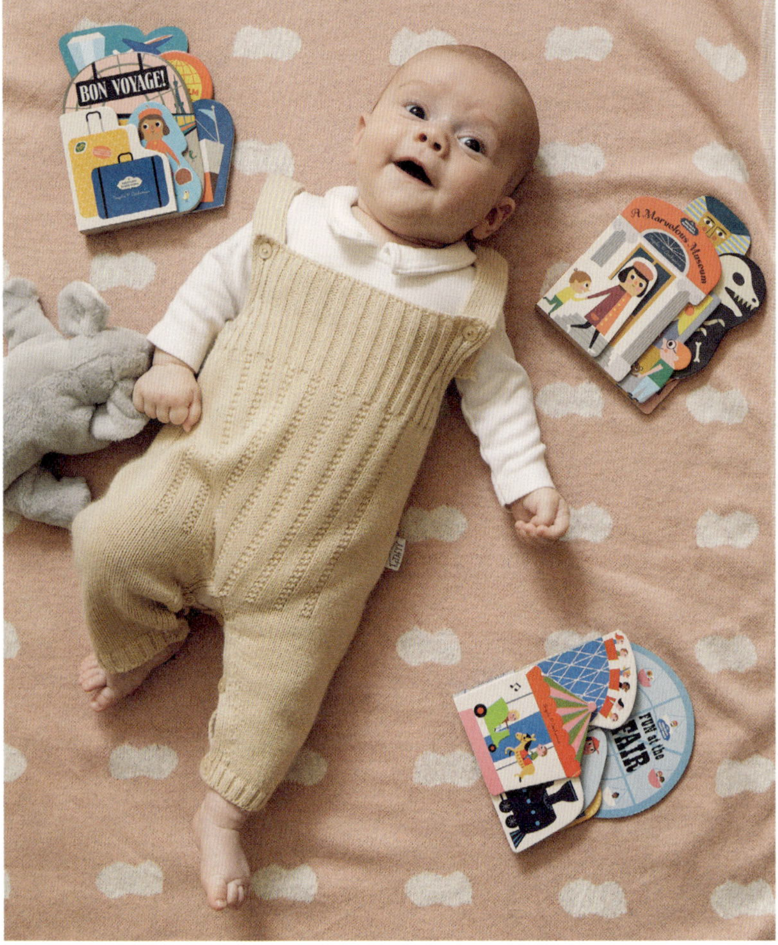
BON VOYAGE!

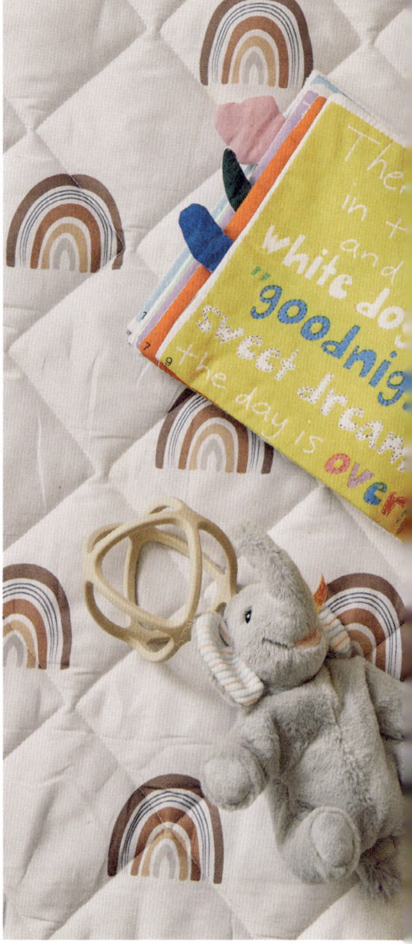

As You GROW
GUESS HOW MUCH I LOVE YOU
Sam McBratney
Anita Jeram

M. SASEK
This is Britain
UNIVERSE
UNIVERSE
This is Ireland
M. SASEK
UNIVERSE
This is London
M. SASEK
LARS JANSSON
MOOMIN: THE COMPLETE LARS JANSSON COMIC STRIP
D+Q
WANG
PRIDE & PREJUDICE
chronicle books
COZY CLASSICS
JANE AUSTEN'S
PRIDE & PREJUDICE

NOOK
6

KIDS

PETER RABBIT'S
Mother Goose Treasury
One Morning in Maine
The Very Hungry Caterpillar
Children's Bible
Usborne

Lions, Rainbows, and Trucks, Oh My!

Book nooks for kids are the most fun to style! You can get creative with the design and playful with the color scheme. Choose a theme, any theme, and run with it. Here are a few to get your wheels turning: dinosaurs; the animal kingdom (or some branch of it: jungle animals, woodland creatures, bugs); planes, trains, and automobiles; fairies; outer space; rainbow (or a single color). And don't feel limited to one theme! Kids are creative. They might want trucks *and* aliens.

If they're old enough, it can be fun to involve your little one in the design process. Ask them questions: What's their favorite book? What's their favorite color? Do they have a vision for their book nook? You never know what their little minds will dream up.

Start their library with on-theme books and then let it grow from there. For an animal-themed children's book nook, stock the shelves with *Brown Bear, Brown Bear* by Bill Martin Jr., and *A Stone Sat Still* by Brendan Wenzel. For an animal-themed middle-grade library, try *The One and Only Ivan* by Katherine Applegate, *A Wolf Called Wander* by Rosanne Parry, and *Mrs. Frisby and the Rats of NIMH* by Robert C. O'Brien.

The new Encyclopedia of the HORSE
DK
THE INVENTION OF HUGO CABRET
Frigidaire

Small Spaces for Small Humans

Kid-friendly book nooks can be squeezed into small spaces—that awkward gap at the end of a bed or a corner beneath a slanted ceiling. With some inventive thinking, you can turn those areas into cozy reading nooks that are actually the perfect size for small humans! Add some cushions, blankets, and stuffed animals, and bam! It's a comfy nook that encourages reading. Bonus points if you can fit a minifridge somewhere in your space. Kids *love* a minifridge.

"WE DO NOT SEE THINGS AS THEY ARE, WE SEE THINGS AS WE ARE."
BIRMINGHAM MUSEUM OF ART
14
ST. PAUL AND THE Broken Bones
A BENEFIT CONCERT
ROBERT SPOTSWOOD
JAMEY JOHNSON
TUSCALOOSA
SPECIAL
LIMITED
NASHVILLE
HUNTSVILLE
GUNTERSVILLE
ONEONTA
GADSDEN
VOTE FOR
POOL RULES
TAROT
MEDIUM
Family
Blokus
Scattergories
BYE, FELICIA!
CODENAMES
SCRABBLE
MONOPOLY
PLINKO
BINGO
Cards Against Humanity
Heads
LONDON
INCANTATIONS
Leonardo da Vinci

Colors and Games

Use bright, saturated colors to prevent a book nook from feeling too serious or mature. The royal blue bunk beds on page 60 add a youthful punch of color. In this nook, the mix of blue, hot pink, and red is happy and energetic. Vibrant or primary colors are fun for kids, and you can bring in these shades via furniture and décor if you don't want to commit to paint.

In this nook, notice that the bookshelves are stacked with more than just books; board games offer visual diversity when stacked among spines. Break up the verticality of books with some horizontal boxes. (Anything you can do to get your kids into their designated reading space helps, right?) Family-friendly games like Apples to Apples, Scattergories, and Monopoly make this a catchall playroom that can be used for gathering, relaxing, playing games, and reading.

Fun and Funky Seating

Spruce up your kid's library with seating options that encourage lounging. Having multiple places to perch creates a space where kids can gather with friends to play a board game or stretch out and relax with their favorite book. Bean bags, poufs, ottomans, loveseats, blow-up chairs, hammocks, and hanging chairs are fabulous options for kids and teenagers. The funkier and less "adult" the seating, the better. Add a lava lamp and a shag rug, and you'll be parent of the year.

CAKE BIBLE
METROPOLITAN HOME
DECORATING IN DETAIL
FORTUNY
VICTORIA HAGAN
DESIGNERS AT HOME
THE COMPLEAT SQUASH
HOUSE & GARDEN BOOK OF STYLE
The Joy of Decorating
BEAUTIFUL

For a one-of-a-kind piece that any kid would love, convert an old armoire into a secret reading spot. With a small sheepskin rug and a couple of pillows, this is the coziest, most covetable book nook for kids. Talk about inventive thinking!

For a stylish book nook that's still kid-friendly, look to vintage items. Go thrifting and search for old-timey books, games, and toys, which instantly add charm to any space. Old-fashioned games and books of a bygone era inspire creativity and imagination. Pop-up books can be left open and displayed as art or stashed on a shelf as a surprise for your kids to discover later.

OTTOLENGHI SIMPLE

CHAD ROBERTSON
TARTINE BOOK Nº3
CHRONICLE BOOKS

NOMA
René Redzepi

waste not
james beard foundation

POLPO
A VEN

NOOK 7

COOK BOOK

NOPI
YOTAM OTTOLENGHI • RAMAEL SCULLY

Funke with Parla **AMERICAN** SFOGLINO

SCHOTT'S FOOD & DRINK MISCELLANY
BEN SCHOTT
WABI-SABI WELCOME
JULIE POINTER ADAMS
The GOURMET FARMER
EVANS HADDOW O'MEARA
CHAD ROBERTSO
TARTINE BOOK №3
TURSHEN
Small Victories
GRAANMARKT 13
SEPPE NOBELS
EVERYTHING I WANT TO EAT
Koslow
Easy Weekends
FOOD BY NEIL PERRY
THEO RANDALL
THE DELI Italian Cookbook
HILDEBRAND & KENEDY
THE GEOMETRY OF PASTA
ROBITSCHEK

Cooking by Hand   Paul Bertolli

NOPI   YOTAM OTTOLENGHI · RAMAEL SCULLY

ITALIAN Regional Cooking   Ada Boni

LORENZO DA PONTE
ITALIAN LIBRARY

Artusi   Science in the Kitchen and the Art of Eating Well

BLAIS — Try This at Home — Recipes From My Head To Your Plate

MARTIN MORALES — CEVICHE — Peruvian Kitchen

BLACK SEA   CAROLINE EDEN

Go Monochrome

Make space in your kitchen or dining area for a beautiful and inspiring cookbook nook. These days, cookbooks are some of the most vibrant and eye-catching books on the market, so they make magnificent décor pieces—especially when grouped together or styled with dishware.

An all-white cookbook nook is like a little black dress. It's easy to style and fits nearly any home aesthetic, from rustic farmhouse to chic and modern. For a more natural look, style a painted wooden hutch with stacks of white bowls, plates, and glassware in textured materials, like unglazed or mottled ceramic, and add cookbooks with white- and neutral-colored spines. For a sleeker look, opt for smooth materials like marble and glass to complement the cookbooks. Add pops of navy blue or black via table linens or serveware for contrast, if you desire.

If white isn't your thing, create a monochromatic look in any color you choose—all blue, all pink, all black! A single colorway makes a memorable décor moment, and it's fun to collect cookbooks based on color—you'll end up with books you might not have otherwise purchased and delicious recipes you might not have otherwise tried.

WABI-SABI WELCOME
The GOURMET FARMER
EVANS HADDOW O'MEARA
TARTINE BOOK Nº3
Small Victories
GRAANMARKT 13
SEPPE NOBELS
EVERYTHING I WANT TO EAT
Kaslow
Easy Weekends
FOOD BY NEIL PERRY
THE GEOMETRY OF PASTA
THE DELI
Italian
Cookbook
NOPI
ITALIAN Regional Cooking
Ada Boni
ROBITSCHEK

Add Visual Interest

Style multicolor bookshelves for a vibrant, happy aesthetic in your kitchen or to match a mishmash of dishware. Brightly colored book spines—or blocks of colored pages—add flair. Intermingle them with blue, pink, green, and yellow kitchen accessories for a room that bursts with joy. Alternating cookbooks arranged upright and laid flat underneath mixing bowls and coffee mugs creates different visual levels on your shelves.

Vintage cookbooks are a delight to collect and add interest to any kitchen or dining room. If you're lucky enough to inherit old cookbooks from a family member, dust them off and exhibit them proudly! Showcase vintage cookbooks together, or mix in one or two with your more recently published cookbooks.

Tear out a favorite recipe from a vintage cookbook or cooking pamphlet and hang it on your fridge, tack it to your wall, or frame it and display it on your kitchen shelf. This adds instant character to your space and will surely be a conversation starter at dinner parties. Or take this idea to the next level and paper your walls entirely in vintage cookbook pages. Voilà: custom, one-of-a-kind wallpaper! (This idea would also work well in a pantry, powder room, or other small space. Or try it as an accent wall.)

WE LOVE madeleines
CHOCOLATE CHIP COOKIES
kitchen confidant
The Modern Family Cook Book
BY META GIVEN
FERGUSON
Mabu Mabu
Nornie Bero
THE NEW YORK TIMES COOK BOOK
Craig Claiborne
Harper & Row
CZECHOSLOVAK COOKBOOK • BRIZOVA
PRIX : 3 FR.
CUISINONS
L'AUVERGNE
REVUE MENSUELLE DE LA MAISON
DE LA CUISINE ET DES ARTS MENAGERS
Tivoli Audio
MODEL ONE
BLACK SEA
CAROLINE EDEN

NIK SHARMA'S Most-Used Cookbooks

"The most treasured cookbooks in my library are the ones I turn to again and again. They've either taught me something new or inspired me to cook. Nowadays, they're not in the best condition; they're stained and dog-eared, and some pages, I must admit, have tears. This isn't because I don't care for them but rather the exact opposite: these cookbooks get used the most."

Rose Levy Beranbaum, *The Pie and Pastry Bible*

Monisha Bharadwaj, *The Indian Cooking Course*

Helen Goh and Yotam Ottolenghi, *Sweet*

Diana Henry, *Simple*

Nigella Lawson, *How to Eat*

Travis Lett, *Gjelina*

Hetty McKinnon, *To Asia with Love*

Claudia Roden, *A Book of Middle Eastern Food*

Lindsey Shere, *Chez Panisse Desserts*

Nigel Slater, *Notes from the Larder*

NIK SHARMA is the molecular biologist turned author, photographer, and cook behind *Nik Sharma Cooks/A Brown Table* and *The Flavor Files* newsletter. Sharma's work has garnered multiple awards, and he was named a Trailblazer in Food by the IACP. His first book, *Season*, was a James Beard Award and IACP Award finalist. His second cookbook, *The Flavor Equation*, was a James Beard Award, IACP Award, and British Guild of Food Writers Award finalist and winner of the silver medal from the German Academy of Gastronomy. His third cookbook, *Veg-Table*, focuses on applying science to vegetable cooking for quicker and more flavorful meals. He lives in Los Angeles.

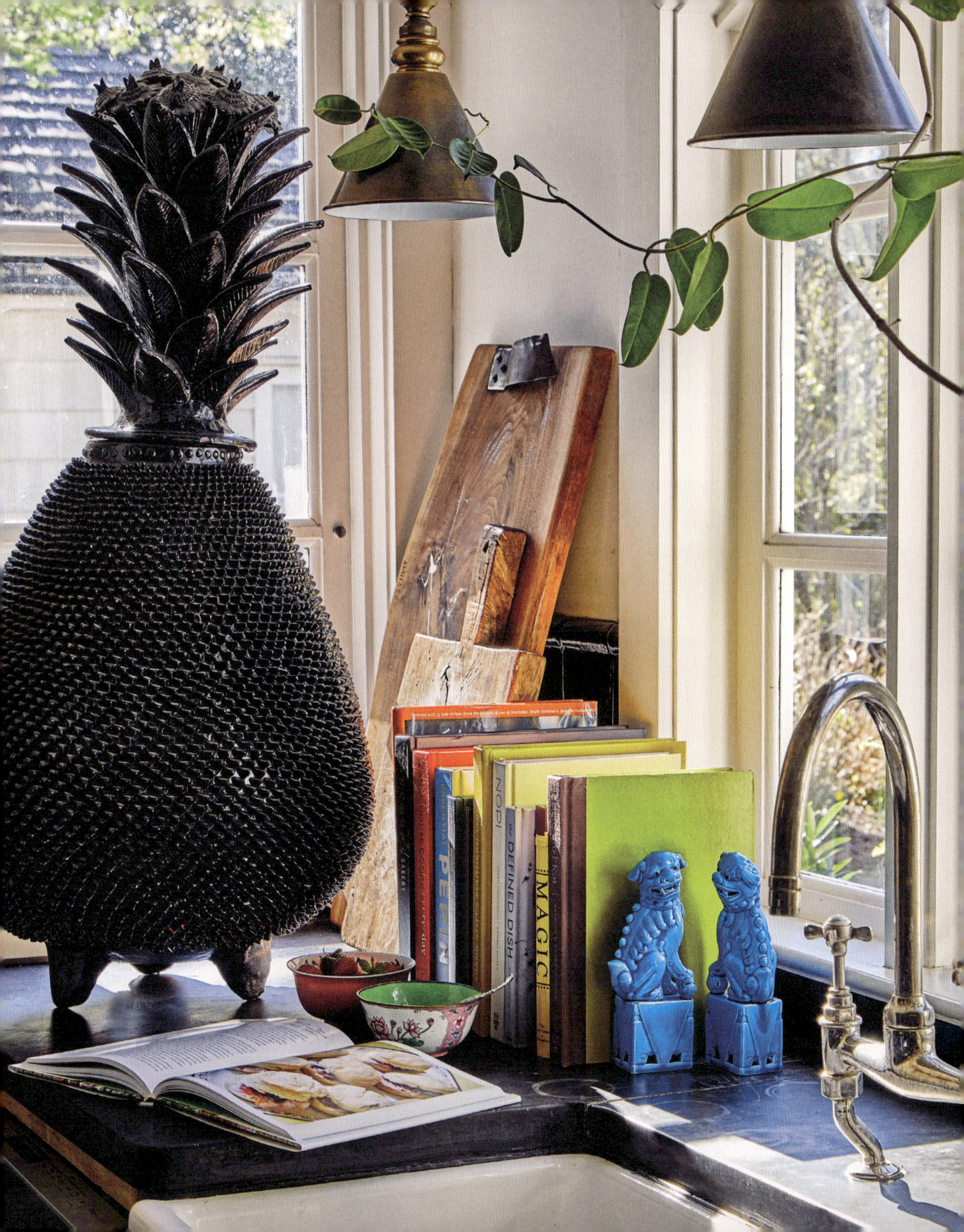
PEPIN
NOPI
the DEFINED DISH
MAGIC

NOOK
8

BAR

DOLIN
VERMOUTH
BRUCATO
AMARO
THE DELI
Italian
Cookbook
ITALIAN Regional Cooking
Ada Boni
NOPI
OTTOLENGHI SIMPLE
TARTINE BOOK Nº3
CEVICHE
pork
D.I.Y. DELICIOUS
SPRITZ

The Setup

A home bar should feature your favorite cocktail books and cookbooks, along with all the liquors, equipment, and other provisions you need to mix up a tasty libation. A cart, a bookcase, a cabinet, or even the corner of your kitchen countertop can be converted into a mini bar with a covetable cocktail book nook. No matter your space, the setup is the same.

Glassware and bar equipment can be quite beautiful on their own and act as a good starting point for setting up your nook. If you have the space, display a variety of glassware, from champagne flutes to rocks, martini, wine, and coupe glasses. Keep in mind that a hodgepodge of glassware—different shapes of cut crystal, or a rainbow of colored glasses—is often more fun to look at than a cohesive set. Stock crucial equipment like a cocktail shaker, barspoon, pitcher, and jigger.

Next, add drink supplies. Cover your bases with go-to liquors, bitters, and mixers, and you'll be ready to whip up a tipple. Keep a bowl of citrus nearby—lemons, limes, oranges, and grapefruit are essential for making cocktails.

A critical step: Enhance your bar nook with cocktail books. Petite drink books like *The Ultimate Bar Book* by Mittie Hellmich, *Tequila Mockingbird* by Tim Federle, and *Kindred Spirits* by Steph Wahler fit nicely on smaller carts and in liquor cabinets. Larger cocktail books like *Death & Co* by Alex Day, David Kaplan, and Nick Fauchald and *Raising the Bar* by Brett Adams and Jacob Grier can make handsome statements if you have the room. Stack them horizontally underneath a vintage ashtray or shapely decanter, or shelve them vertically, propped up against a stone serving platter or wooden cutting board.

Last but not least, adorn your bar cart with a vase of dried flowers, which will last for months, or assorted objects, like a beautiful geode or agate slice, a print or figurine that caught your eye, or any quirky souvenir from your travels. These accent pieces are perfect cocktail-hour conversation starters and add personality to your home bar.

FOOD & WINE
COCKTAILS
LAZOR
HOW TO DRINK FRENCH
PARR AND MACKAY
SECRETS OF THE SOMMELIERS
FROM CROOK TO COOK
CAN I MIX YOU A DRINK?
T-PAIN
BARTELS
the bloody mary
NEWMAN
Cocktails with a Twist
ARE YOU THERE GOD? IT'S ME, MARGARITA
FEDERLE
PARIS
PARIS COCKTAILS
GIN COCKTAILS
STUART WALTON
NIGHTCAP
KARA NEWMAN

BRUCATO
AMARO
WOODLANDS
ST-GERMAIN
UXARDO
HENDRICK
GIN
Amaro
APERITIF
Wine Pairing Party
SICILY
Sicily
Never Let Me Go
Kazuo Ishiguro
THE FAMILY
STOLEN LIVES
THE CHEESE BOARD DECK
Vietnamese Home Cooking
SHELF LOVE
SUNDAY SUPPERS AT LUCQUES
SUZANNE GOIN
THE HOMEBREW HANDBOOK
THUG KITCHEN
KATZ
ART of FERMENTATION

Themes for Every Style

Bar carts and liquor cabinets are self-contained spaces that can be equally practical and stylish. They present an opportunity to get creative with a theme: For a subtle French flair, stock bottles of Lillet and St-Germain, etched coupe glasses, a bowl of lemons, a vase of fresh or dried lavender, and *Aperitif* by Rebekah Peppler. For a tropical bar nook, display *Tiki* by Shannon Mustipher, and *Smuggler's Cove* by Martin and Rebecca Cate. Add a potted monstera plant, brightly colored glassware, and a pineapple cocktail shaker to round out the look. And make sure to have plenty of rum on hand! A nonalcoholic bar cart might feature booze-free spirits and *Good Drinks* by Julia Bainbridge. Your bar cart might revolve around a specific color; a specific liquor or drink—tequila, say, or spritzes; or a specific holiday like Christmas or Halloween.

Make your bar nook kid-friendly by adding smoothie or milkshake supplies. A bowl of fruit, colorful swizzle straws, and *Feel Good Smoothies* by Sandra Wu create a darling—and healthy—nook for kids. Classic, diner-style milkshake cups with long spoons and a jar of maraschino cherries create a retro vibe that kids will love. Add a couple kiddie cookbooks, like Melissa Clark's *Kid in the Kitchen*, and this becomes a fun place to browse recipes—or come up with your own.

A small console, cabinet, or sideboard can serve as an excellent home bar. Having cabinet doors that close allows you to store excess glassware, equipment, or bottles of liquor out of sight. (If you have kids or teenagers in the house, you might even consider a cabinet that locks.) Stack your cocktail books on top of or beneath the piece of furniture—wherever there's a bit of space.

Classic Margarita with Tajín Rim

Nothing pairs better with a beach read than a margarita. Serve up two of these refreshing cocktails with some chips and guacamole; head to the beach, pool, porch, park, or anywhere outside; and bring your book of choice for a leisurely afternoon of lounging in the sun. Need a recommendation? Try *Barbarian Days* by William Finnegan, *Beach Read* by Emily Henry, or *Lonesome Dove* by Larry McMurtry.

MAKES 2 DRINKS

Tajín, for the glasses

Salt, for the glasses and to taste

3 lime wedges

4 oz [120 ml] tequila

2 oz [60 ml] freshly squeezed lime juice

1 oz [30 ml] Cointreau

Simple syrup, to taste

On a plate wider than the rim of your rocks glasses, mix one part Tajín and one part salt. Run one lime wedge around the rims of the glasses, then dip the rims in the Tajín–salt mixture. Fill the glasses with ice.

In an ice-filled cocktail shaker, add the tequila, lime juice, Cointreau, one or two dashes of simple syrup to taste, and a sprinkle of salt to taste. Shake for 15 seconds, or until chilled. Strain into the glasses. Garnish each glass with a lime wedge and enjoy!

JULIANNA McINTOSH'S Go-To Cocktail Books

"Are you ready to raise a glass and elevate your bar cart? This carefully curated collection of ten drink-related books is here to help you quench your thirst and upgrade your homemade cocktails, mocktails, or low-ABV drinks just in time for happy hour. With their mouthwatering beverage photography and informative home bartending tips, these books will help you step into the wonderful world of beverages. Cheers to sipping, learning, and elevating your drink game!"

Talia Baiocchi and Leslie Pariseau, *Spritz*

Benny Briga and Adeena Sussman, *Gazoz*

Harry Craddock, *The Savoy Cocktail Book*

Natasha David, *Drink Lightly*

Alex Day, David Kaplan, and Nick Fauchald, *Cocktail Codex*

Emma Janzen, *The Bartender's Manifesto*

Julianna McIntosh, *Pretty Simple Cocktails*

Rebekah Peppler, *Apéritif*

Robert Simonson, *Mezcal and Tequila Cocktails*

David Wondrich, *Imbibe!*

JULIANNA McINTOSH is the creator of *Join Jules*, an online platform dedicated to making craft beverages accessible to all. What started as an online beverage project evolved into a thriving community of over a million followers, where drink enthusiasts come together to learn, create, and share so that we all can enjoy the happiest of hours in the comfort of our own homes. Focusing on seasonal ingredients, inviting recipes, and a welcoming tone, *Join Jules* brings people together—from what we're drinking, to where we're going, and how we're entertaining.

NUMBER TWO JOY STREET
APPLETON
THE BEST OF THE WORLD'S CLASSICS
I GREECE
II ROME
THE BEST OF THE WORLD'S CLASSICS
THE RING OF THE LÖWENSKÖLDS
SELMA LAGERLÖF
THE GENERAL'S RING
CHARLOTTE LÖWENSKÖLD
ANNA SVÄRD
The Further Adventures of Nils
Selma Lagerlöf

NOOK 9

THE COLLECTOR

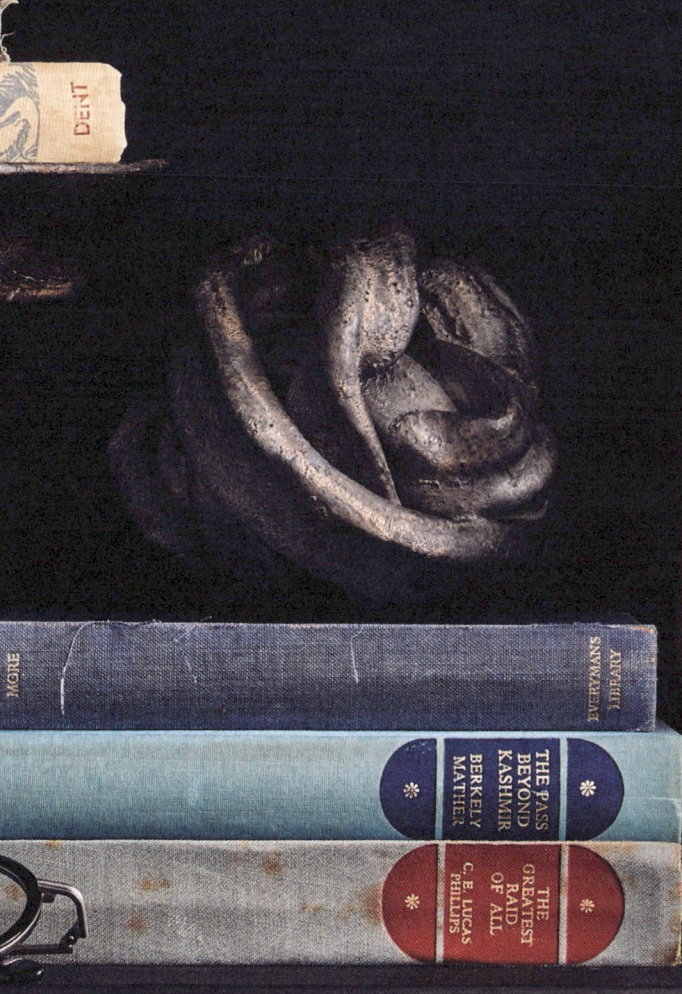

Hobbies and Collections

This type of nook serves to celebrate your hobby, whatever that may be, via books and décor (and books *as* décor!). No matter your niche—be it music, golf, woodworking, cooking—show it off. Books are one of the easiest ways to do this.

The design of a hobbyist's book nook depends, of course, on its owner. Into sports? Fill your nook with books like *The Mamba Mentality* by Kobe Bryant and *Shoe Dog* by Phil Knight, along with memorabilia such as iconic posters, framed jerseys, autographed balls, elusive baseball cards, bobbleheads from memorable games, helmets of favorite players, and pennants of beloved teams.

If you're an angler, framed fishing flies (which can be so beautiful!), plus books like *A River Runs Through It* by Norman Maclean and *The History of Fly-Fishing in Fifty Flies* by Ian Whitelaw set the stage for a fishing-themed nook. Or maybe you love birding. Or, like this homeowner, you collect hats. Whatever your thing, design a nook that displays relevant books and objects with care, and showcases your collection and passion proudly.

A.S. BYATT
Possession
Arabian Sands
COLOUR
HOMELANDS
TIMOTHY GARTON ASH
MOBY DICK
SPLENDOR SOLIS
ANDRÉ BRETON NADJA
SPLENDOR SOLIS
REMARKABLE BOOKS
ABY WARBURG
BILDERATLAS MNEMOSYNE
ALEXANDRIE LA DIVINE
ALEXANDRIE LA DIVINE
MARCEL PROUST
DU CÔTÉ DE CHEZ SWANN
LEONOR FINI
CONSTANTIN JELENSKI
LEONOR FINI
C.G. JUNG
THE RED BOOK
LOCK & Co
HATTERS
St. James's Street
LONDON

Stags Leap
Stags Leap
Stags Leap
CONTENTS
6 MAGNUMS
Stags Leap
ROCK POSTERS
NOMA
COCO
MARQUE
BURMA
SLOW FIRES
ZAHAV
CAMINO
SILVER OAK
FOOD
PERU
BOHEMIAN

Read On, Rock On

Perfect inspiration for a music aficionado, this book nook places the interests of its owner front and center. Clearly, this homeowner is a music lover through and through. Just look at that collection of guitars!

Browse a bookcase and you'll immediately get a sense of what someone is interested in. These particular shelves stock books of all types, not just music books. There are travel books, cookbooks, and books on notable chefs, restaurants, and vineyards. Books on music and photography complete the collection, while wine crates stashed on top of the shelves house records. (Vinyl and vino, what a combo!)

When designing your hobby nook—or really any nook for that matter—don't feel as if you must adhere so closely to one theme that you can't introduce books on other topics. We all have a wide range of interests; your book nook should reflect that, especially if it's designed purely for your own enjoyment.

Floating Shelves

Here, a homeowner stores their cookbook collection (with a few music books mixed in!) on a floating bookshelf. A nifty storage solution, floating shelves, once loaded with books, disappear entirely, creating what looks like very tall, freestanding stacks of books. Nail them into the wall for support, and then pile on the books to achieve the intended effect.

Floating shelves are particularly useful in small spaces and rooms with a lot of furniture or items competing for your attention. A hidden bookshelf means one fewer thing to look at.

HALLOWEEN
DECORATIVE ART 60s
BREAKFAST
EVERYDAY SLOW COOKER
SERIOUSLY DELICIOUS
THE BLUES
SOUL
FEEL GOOD FOOD
BOWIE WENDY LEIGH
Second Helpings
Off the Eaten Path
LIGHTEN UP, AMERICA!
Gluten-Free Cookbook
SLO DINNERS
Staff Favorites Potluck
Potluck
PASTA
Wood-Fired Pizza Oven
SPANISH FLAVORS
MINIMALIST KITCHEN
GLOBAL KITCHEN
SUNDAY SUPPERS
JERUSALEM
OTTOLENGHI
THE VEGAN 8
THE Southern Living PARTY COOKBOOK
HEADLANDS
DECORATING BOOK
GLUTEN-FREE BAKING
SERIOUSLY DELICIOUS
TEXAS
Soul
TODD RICHARDS
Essential Emeril
THE SOUTHERN BAKER
NO TASTE LIKE HOME
Site Matters
Colin McCahon: Artist
COOKIES
CAST IRON NATION
everyday VEGETARIAN
THE SOUTHERN VEGETABLE BOOK
On the Road Again
Off the Eaten Path
NEW YORK IN THE SIXTIES
THE MINIMALIST KITCHEN
Dinner Made Simple
ULTIMATE BBQ
Seaside Interiors
ALABAMA BIRDS
EASY-CARE PLANTINGS
WEST COAST
UNITED TASTES
the new classics
MAD DELICIOUS

- DICKENS'S COMPLETE WORKS — UNCOMMERCIAL TRAVELLER — HARPERS
- ROEBUCK / LONSDALE — **FORAGED FLORA**
- **FOREST SCHOOL FOR GROWN-UPS** — IRVINE — CHRONICLE BOOKS
- RIX — *The Art of the Plant World* — THE OVERLOOK PRESS
- ROBBINS — everyday radiance
- Claudia Swan — THE CL... PLANTS

NOOK
10

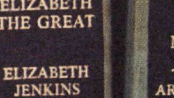

THE
GARDENER

THE GRUMPY GARD
DECORATING WITH PL
THE HOUSEPLAN
PLANTOPED
MARGOT SHAW
PLANT RECIPE BOOK
A PLACE TO CALL HOME
GARDEN BOOK
Southern Living
AtelierAM

ITALIAN VILLAS AND THEIR GARDENS
Timeless Landscape Design
CAPABILITY BROWN
VINTAGE ROSES
italian country living
SECOND BLOOM
HUNTER

No need to hide gardening equipment if its weathered appearance adds charm, like this vintage hoe. Pick up a used trowel or shovel, collect old woven baskets, and display secondhand gardening books. Add an apron, and you have a delightfully rustic book nook.

Gardening tools function in more ways than one. Use them as décor in your book nook; for example, a fancy spray bottle looks fantastic sitting atop a pile of books, and the tiniest terra-cotta pot acts as a paperweight.

A Bucolic Nook

Gardening, like reading, is a hobby that brings joy, inspiration, and peace. Even though both are solitary activities, they lead to connection and community. When you meet a fellow gardener, as when you meet a fellow book lover, your mutual interest can create an instant connection. A garden book nook combines two enjoyable hobbies and creates a space to revel in both. Imagine how much contentment such a space might evoke!

This particular garden book nook (pages 100 to 102) is a corner carved out in the homeowner's mudroom. If you're lucky enough to have a designated area to devote to a garden book nook—such as a greenhouse, a shed, or a mudroom like this one—take full advantage of it. But even if you don't, you can easily create a nook on a table, on a bench, or in another corner of your home. Find a sunny spot near the entrance to your garden, on a patio or balcony, or simply beneath a window. Position a table, bookshelf, or piece of furniture as a place to stash your books and as an anchor, grounding the space.

Collect and display garden- and nature-themed books on and around your anchor piece. Is your green book nook focused on gardening, farming, flowers, houseplants, climate change, or sustainability? Or all the above? Curate your book collection accordingly.

Houseplant Haven

Living in an urban environment doesn't preclude you from having a garden (or enjoying a garden book nook). It might have to be indoors, but no matter! Caring for a throng of houseplants has benefits similar to gardening outside. Houseplants aid mental health, purify the air, add beauty, and encourage mindfulness and a connection with nature.

Bookshelves are perfect spots to showcase a collection of houseplants, like this long, low shelf in front of a sunny window. Mingle potted plants and stacks of books together. Succulents, cacti, snake plants, pothos, and monstera are hearty houseplants that will add healthy doses of greenery, freshness, and visual diversity alongside your books' spines. Hang a couple plants from the ceiling and place a one-off houseplant, like an orchid, on your coffee table or end table alongside *Plantopedia* by Lauren Camilleri and Sophia Kaplan or *You Grow, Gurl!* by Christopher Griffin.

Empty vases also make beautiful décor for a book nook. If you feel inclined, start a collection! Place vases of different shapes and sizes on top of stacked books, or use them as bookends (filled with sand or pebbles for more weight).

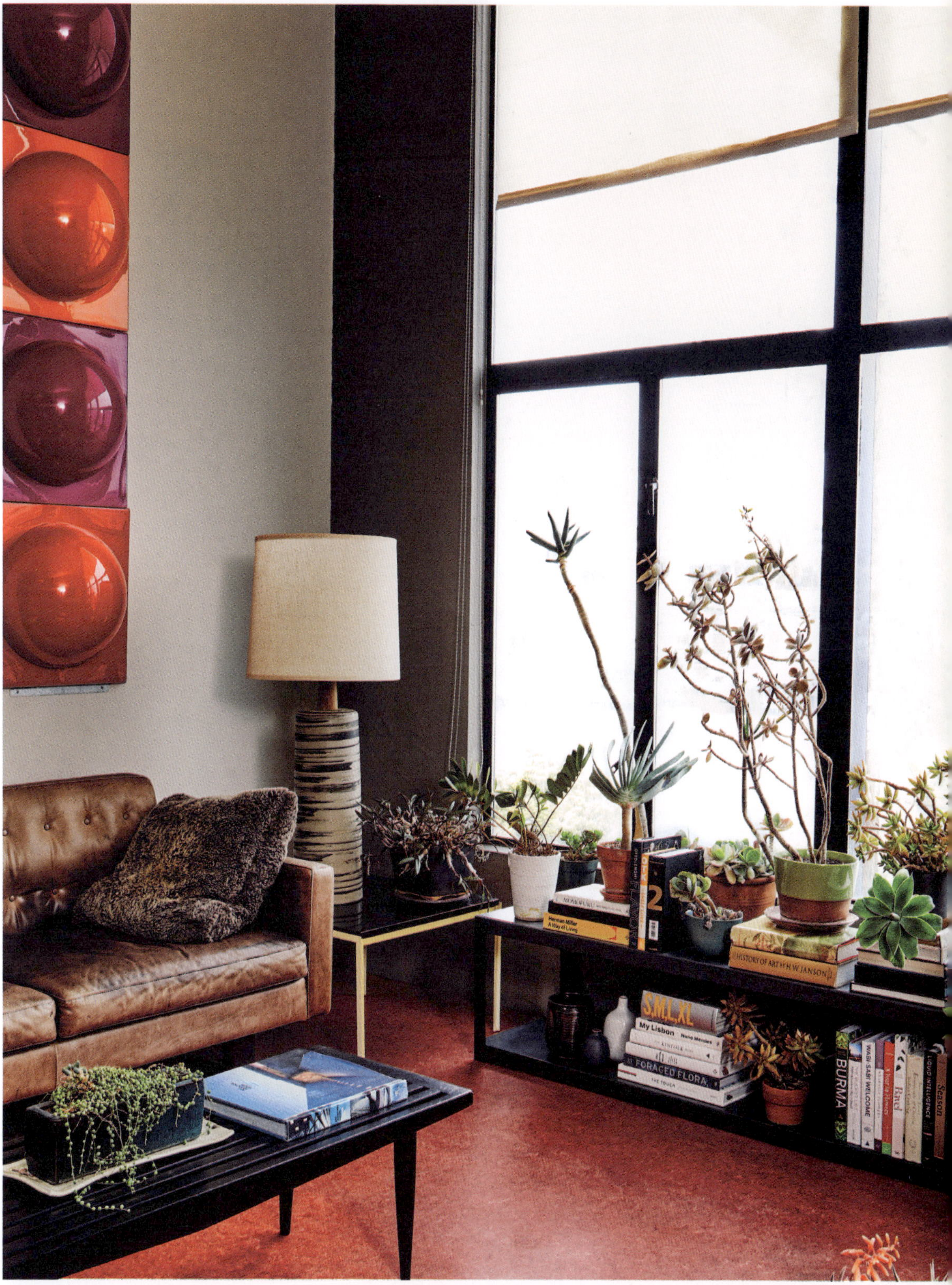

OTTOLENGHI
FLAVOR
OTK
SHELF LOVE
2
TASCHEN
S,M,L,XL
My Lisbon
Nuno Mendes
THE KINFOLK HOME
FORAGED FLORA
THE TOUCH

H.W. JANSON
BURMA
THE BUCKET LIST
1000 Adventures Big & Small
WABI-SABI WELCOME
WEARABLE FLOWERS
A Year in Flowers
Bavel
Marcella Hazan
Essentials of Classic Italian Cooking
LIQUID INTELLIGENCE
Season

LAMBERTO VITALI

GIORGIO MORANDI

TERZA EDIZIONE

EDIZIONI DEL MILIONE

Paul Klee

PERFECT IMPERFECT

Karen McCarthy / Sharyn Cairns / Glen Proebstel

HATJE CANTZ

Antoinette Le Normand-Romain
Christina Buley-Uribe

Auguste Rodin
Drawings & Watercolours

IMPRESSIONISM

VAN GOGH

CÉZANNE

MORGAN FALCONER

NOOK
11

THE
ARTIST

ISABEY 6234 PETIT

INTING BEYOND POLLOCK

GREAT HOLLYWOOD MOVIES
INTIMACY
OTHER CRITERIA
SERRA
FEMALE TROUBLE
SCHIRMER ART BOOKS
mel's music icons
PAPERBOY
ROBERT FREEMAN
BEATLES
THE ROCK 'N' ROLL YEARS
CRESCENT
THE BEATLES ANTHOLOGY
THE GENIUS OF PRINCE
andy Warhol
Andy WARHOL 365 Takes
i sold Andy Warhol (too soon)
THE ANDY WARHOL DIARIES
PRINCE THE BEAUTIFUL ONES
SPACE ODYSSEY
THE COMPLETE DAVID BOWIE
Bowie/Collector
PRINT BY STICKER MUSIC ICONS
BOWIE
BOWIE IS INSIDE
ELVIS PRESLEY
GRACELAND
ELVIS AT 21 NEW YORK TO MEMPHIS
ALFRED WERTHEIMER

Nooks for All Artists

The label *artist* encompasses a variety of vocations—painter, sculptor, musician, actor, dancer, photographer, designer—the list goes on. Therefore, an *artist nook* is up to some interpretation. A collection of artsy volumes on Ruth Asawa, Richard Mayhew, Georgia O'Keefe, and other icons? That's an artist nook. A corner piled with books on theater and treasured Broadway *Playbills*? You bet, that's an artist nook. A case teeming with books on music—the science, the stars, the untold stories? You guessed it—that's an artist nook too.

In this particular art-themed book nook, a music superfan displays their assortment of music books and art pieces in a Cubitec shelving unit. Tomes of all the greats live here, from Elvis to David Bowie, and Prince to the Beatles. Colorful ceramics and a Magis green Puppy chair by Eero Aarnio add whimsy to the space. A bust of Prince by Troy Gua is complemented by other dolls and figurines found at the MoMA store and on Etsy. (Museum stores are unsung heroes! They reliably stock some of the best, most surprising, giftable finds.) It's a mishmash of pop star memorabilia. The books play more of a supporting role here—they're not the main attraction in this alcove, but they're necessary to the design. Their mixed orientations add dynamism, and the book stacks create varying levels on which to showcase the fun collectibles.

Mix the Unexpected

Here's another interpretation of an artist nook—one that pops with reddish orange, acid green, bright white, and brown-black, not to mention a mixture of unique shapes, textures, and levels.

Beneath the painting *Umari Rockhole* by Ronnie Tjampitjinpa sits a reddish-orange bench that picks up on the concentric lines in the painting. Art and design books arranged atop the bench cover subjects such as the work of French industrial designer Philippe Starck, English designer Thomas Heatherwick, and American fashion editor Diana Vreeland.

Fine art and high fashion books are usually hefty and make for a sophisticated and stately display; face their gorgeously designed covers outward. The subtle pyramid shape created by the varying levels of these books is not only pleasing but also leads the eye to the art above.

Complete with a cowhide rug, sizable floor lamp, and funky lounge chair, this thoughtfully designed book nook boasts an attention-grabbing mélange of form and color.

WILLIAM KLEIN
IN THE AMERICAN WEST
SCAVULLO
BRAVOS
Heatherwick
MONDINO
STARCK
IN FOCUS
DIANA VREELAND THE EYE HAS TO TRAVEL
popart style
CURATORIAL INTERVENTION
Tortured Artists
SHOCK VALUE
CURATORIAL ACTIVISM
LOFTS
PREFAB
NEW ITALIAN DESIGN
Modernism Rediscovered

curb your enthusiasm: The Book
HELMUT NEWTON
HELMUT NEWTON
HEAVEN TO HELL
DAVID LACHAPELLE
LaChapelle Land
Photographs by David LaChapelle
Warhol
fabricated
OVER 100 WORKS
Warhol
fabricated
THE WES ANDERSON COLLECTION

A Little Avant-Garde

For an avant-garde art nook, collect modern art books and books with loud, bold covers. Exhibiting these books on a piece of Lucite furniture allows them to shine: To the human eye, the furniture disappears, and the colorful hardcovers anchor your sightline. Here, the Lucite table offers two levels of display, both used judiciously for eye-catching books: *LaChapelle Land* and *LaChapelle, Heaven to Hell* by David LaChapelle, an American photographer known for fashion photography and celebrity portraits; a book on American filmmaker Wes Anderson; and a collection of photographs by German-Australian photographer Helmut Newton. Knickknacks like an illuminated lightning bolt and plates by Dinosaur Designs contribute to the modern aesthetic. Re-create this voguish nook with bright and colorful, visually arresting contemporary art books stacked on any Lucite furniture—a coffee table, sideboard, or even a pair of chairs would work.

Contrast and the Rule of Threes

This final art nook is perfect for an entryway or foyer. Its composition is similar to that on page 113, with a long, low table hosting art books positioned beneath a piece of art—a photograph titled *Hemi Tuwharerangi Paraha* by Ross T. Smith. Though the photograph is dark and moody and the traditional table is a classic walnut, color abounds in this alcove, thanks to all the books and trinkets. Substantial books with thick spines in bold colors add vibrancy, as does the blue watering can. The single daffodil stem in sunny yellow, though not a permanent fixture, is such a delightful touch. That type of contrast—dark with light, neutral with color, old with new—makes any space more interesting and unique. This transitional nook has contrasts in spades.

A cork tray creates a separate section on the tabletop, dividing it into thirds (threes, and odd numbers in general, are more pleasing to look at). The three stools beneath the table reinforce this division. The homeowner found those stools and the watering can at Target—showcasing another type of contrast (high-market and low) and proving that you don't have to spend significant amounts of money to achieve great style.

HOKIANGA
THE EXHIBITIONIST
Donald Judd Writings
cream
INSIDE ASIA
THE CURIOUS MR SOTTSASS
VERTIGO
PHILIP GUSTON NOW
GUIDE TO ENTERTAINING
THE WORLD WE LIVE IN
Landscape of Transformations
NEW HOUSE BOOK
GUEST

- Pierre Yovanovitch — Interior Architecture
- Silvia Bächli — LIDSCHLAG
- JOAN ALMOND
- Curiosity and Method: Ten Years of Cabinet Magazine
- THE LAND GOD GAVE TO CAIN — HAMMOND INNES

COLORFUL

NOOK 12

TROPICAL HOUSES
HOME A CELEBRATION
THE GREAT BOOK OF JEWELS
Allure Diana Vreeland
RICHARD GILLETTE
THOMAS O'BRIEN
GUCCI
BESTIARY
SPLASH
ENDANGERED TIM FLACH
DEBUTANTES
HOTEL CHIC AT HOME
A Thousand Days of Magic
TRACING ROOTS
GJELINA
BEST OF
Living in the Countryside
PRUNE
SLIM AARONS · LA DOLCE VITA
ULTIMATE BBQ
PLENTY
COMING HOME
Great Stud-Farms of the World
STONE
THE STYLISH LIFE
GLAMOROUS ROOMS
EVOCATIVE INTERIORS
LORENZO CASTILLO
THE COMPLEAT SQUASH
ZUBER
BUNNY MELLON STYLE
MOUNTAIN HOUSES
McALPINE

“The horse.
Here is nobility without
conceit, friendship without
envy, beauty
vanity. A w
yet never a s
ENDANGERED TIM FLACH
GREEK GEMS AND FINGER RINGS
AT HOME
BETH WEBB An Eye for Beauty
BUNNY WILLIAMS' POINT OF VIEW
The Southern Rustic Cabin
NICKY HASLAM
French Style at Home
SALADINO VILLA
AT HOME WITH TOWN & COUNTRY
NEW OLD HOUSE
THE ROMANTIC EGOISTS
MARIO BUATTA
Decorating with Antiques
TextileStyle
ODD NERDRUM
THE HEIGHT of STYLE
MONOGRAMS FOR THE HOME
PERFECT ENGLISH TOWNHOUSE
WINE TOURS
THE WORLD'S GREATEST PLACES
STEVEN GAMBREL
BLUE & WHITE and other stories
the new classics
100 INTERIORS AROUND THE WORLD
NEW ARCHITECTURE OF THE AMERICAN SOUTH
Mykonos
LIVING FLORAL
DESIGN-SPONGE at HOME
CABINETS OF WONDER
MODERN
AN ADVENTUROUS LIFE
A PLACE TO CALL HOME
ARRIVING HOME
In Country Style
LISTEN TO THE LAND
KELLY WEARSTLER
Decorating Secrets
VILLAS OF TUSCANY
INSPIRED BY TRADITION
The Houses of VERANDA
COMING HOME
FRENCH COUNTRY LIVING
FRANCE
METROPOLITAN HOME
GRACIOUS ROOMS
GREAT PAINTINGS OF THE WESTERN WORLD
RELIGION
French Seaside Style
THE NEW OLD HOUSE
STYLE AND SUBSTANCE
WALLS
SO CHIC
SALENTO Style
VALENTINO
KIT KEMP
DECORATE FEARLESSLY!

STYLE BY SALADINO
ZUBER
FARROW&BALL DECORATING with COLOUR
EXOTIC TASTE
AXEL VERVOORDT
GUCCI
ENDANGERED TIM FLACH
envy, beauty
vanity. A w
yet never a s
DECORATING IN DETAIL
CHRISTIAN DIOR: DESIGNER OF DREAMS
Robert Kime
American Modern
PRUNE
Living in the Countryside
ABSOLUTELY BEAUTIFUL THINGS ANNA SPIRO
THE MOST BEAUTIFUL ROOMS IN THE WORLD
SLIM AARONS · LA DOLCE VITA
Oscar de la Renta
Mykonos
MODERN MIX
CABINETS of WONDER
FORM FOLLOWS LIFE
DESIGN-SPONGE at HOME
LIVING FLORAL
ITALIA
SWIMMING POOLS
SUZANNE KASLER SOPHISTICATED SIMPLICITY
MARKHAM ROBERTS
VICTORIA HAGAN INTERIOR PORTRAITS
AN ADVENTUROUS LIFE
A PLACE TO CALL HOME
ARRIVING HOME
LISTEN TO THE LA

TIM STREET-PORTER TROPICAL HOUSES
HOME A CELEBRATION
My Beverly Hills Kitchen ALEX HITZ
THE GREAT BOOK OF JEWELS
Cecil Beaton at Home AN INTERIOR LIFE
Allure Diana Vreeland BULFINCH
FLAIR ANNUAL 1953
The New Eighteenth-Century Home
BESTIARY
BEAUTIFUL
ad hoc at home
SPLASH TIM STREET-PORTER
SOIRÉE Danielle Rollins
THE DECORATED HOME Meg Braff
FLORENCE
SHADES OF GREY
FINDING HOME THE HOUSES OF PURSLEY DIXON
GJELINA
BEST OF
dream homes

Rainbows for the Win

Not only are rainbows inherently joyful, but there's also something so satisfying about color-coding, whether with books, pens, clothes, or calendars. Things look clean and tidy when grouped by shade, creating a sense of calm and order, as if all is right in the world (or at least in your home!).

Sorting books by hue works best against a neutral-colored bookshelf. A black or white background lets the colors pop and creates a striking visual effect. This homeowner constructed black built-in shelves (pages 120 to 123)—perfect for letting book covers stand out.

To organize your books in this fashion, begin by creating a pile of green books, a pile of blue books, and so forth. Having a sense of how many books you own in each colorway allows you to think strategically about the composition of your shelves. Tons of blue books? Divide them into shades: light blue, royal blue, navy. Lots of white books? Use them on multiple shelves throughout the design to punctuate the color.

Consider whether the shelves should progress in a rainbow pattern, whether from left to right or top to bottom. A complete rainbow creates a more playful look, which works well if your house is whimsical and saturated with color, or if you're designing a teenager's room or a bright, happy kitchen. Alternatively, mix up the color groupings on your shelves (for example, instead of a ROYGBIV progression, try

YBGVIRO) for a sophisticated look—a better fit for a modern house, a handsome home office, or an elegant living room.

Rainbow shelves can also serve as a celebratory nod to LGBTQIA+ Pride. Using books to pay homage to those who fought for gay rights, and echoing that celebration with Pride flag–inspired shelves can be a fun way to express remembrance. Incorporate *The Pride Atlas* by Maartje Hensen and *This Book Is Gay* by Juno Dawson, both of which boast colorful covers.

If you're more of a minimalist, try using a limited color scheme in your library, such as an ombré pattern. If ombré isn't your thing, draw on your favorite color combinations to determine a semi-limited palette in which to work, such as red and pink or blue and purple. Look to your existing home décor to inspire a colorful book nook that feels right for your space.

Among color-coded shelves, intersperse beloved trinkets. This homeowner (pages 120 to 123) loves the sea and incorporated beachy objects—shells, dried coral, dried anemones—throughout their books to enliven the display and add visual diversity. Framed and unframed photos and paintings, a petite sculpture, a vase, and a camera complete the vignette.

DECORATING IN DETAIL ALEXA HAMPTON
BEAUTIFUL MARK D. SIKES
Chris Casson Madden A ROOM OF HER OWN
The Meaning of Home

SUZANNE KASLER SOPHISTICATED SIMPLICITY
Southern Style
FIONA BARRATT-CAMPBELL ELEMENTS
SWIMMING POOLS
LISTEN TO THE LAND
VICTORIA HAGAN INTERIOR PORTRAITS
INSPIRED BY TRADITION
VILLAS OF TUSCANY
JOSEPH DIRAND Interior

BETH WEBB An Eye for Beauty
AT HOME
BUNNY WILLIAMS' POINT OF VIEW
A PLACE TO CALL HOME
GREEK GEMS AND FINGER RINGS
AXEL VERVOORDT

Mykonos
A FRENCH COUNTRY HOME
May I Come In? WENDY GOODMAN
BEJEWELED
Michael S. Smith Houses
Cecil Beaton at Home
Allure Diana Vreeland
TROPICAL HOUSES
HOME A CELEBRATION
My Beverly Hills Kitchen ALEX HITZ
THE GREAT BOOK OF JEWELS

Colorful Book Stacks

To achieve a similarly joyful and color-coded look in a smaller nook, stack your books. On a stool, chair, or pedestal, pile your books by color. Assemble them in the order of a rainbow, or create an ombré effect from light to dark. Use just two favorite colors and create color blocks within your stack (five yellow books atop five red books, for example) or alternate colors for a striped stack (white, green, white, green). Both approaches look incredibly stylish and couldn't be easier to pull off.

Style a handsome, neutral stack using only books in muted blues, browns, and creams. For a more haphazard, less intentional look, face some of the pages and some of the spines outward. The styling possibilities are endless, so look around at your current furnishings and décor to determine the right approach for your colorful book nook.

- KIT KEMP *A Living Space*
- VALENTINO AT THE EMPEROR'S TABLE
- SLIM AARONS · ONCE UPON A TIME
- SALENTO Style
- Paris Interiors
- Edible Selby
- One Hundred & One Beautiful Small Towns in Italy
- Mykonos
- May I Come In? Wendy Goodman
- TIM STREET-PORTER Tropical Houses
- HOME: A CELEBRATION
- Cecil Beaton at Home: An Interior Life
- Allure — Diana Vreeland
- FLAIR ANNUAL 1953

JAMISE HARPER'S Most Recommended Diverse Spines

"I strongly believe that reading diverse stories can expand your awareness, help foster empathy, and cultivate opportunities for growth and understanding. This list features my most-often recommended books. They showcase the humanity of Black people and their lived experiences. Whether through storytelling, historical facts, or real events, these books reveal what it means to be Black in America."

James Baldwin, *The Fire Next Time*

Yaa Gyasi, *Homegoing*

Honorée Fanonne Jeffers, *The Love Songs of W. E. B. Du Bois*

Robert Jones Jr., *The Prophets*

Bernice McFadden, *Sugar*

Ann Petry, *The Street*

Claudia Rankine, *Citizen*

Clint Smith, *How the Word Is Passed*

Bryan Stevenson, *Just Mercy*

Jesmyn Ward, *Men We Reaped*

Isabel Wilkerson, *The Warmth of Other Suns*

JAMISE HARPER is the creator of the #diversespines hashtag and the Diverse Spines online book community, which highlights literature by Black women and women of color, as well as *Spines & Vines*, a blog dedicated to book and wine pairings (perfect for book club inspiration!). She is the coauthor (with Jane Mount) of *Bibliophile: Diverse Spines*, a richly illustrated and vastly inclusive collection that uplifts the works of authors who are often underrepresented in the literary world. @spinesvines, @diversespines

Aesop.

ROTHKO
THE COLOR FIELD PAINTINGS

A FRAME FOR LIFE
ILSE CRAWFORD

Tonita & Judge
Edo Craftsmen

Manhattan

REMBRANDT
GEMÄLDE

DRIFT
Volume 10

SUNDAY SUPPERS
KAREN MO

musings of a curious aesthete

Alvar Aalto
Vitra Design Museum

NEUTRAL

NOOK 13

White on white on white creates a super sleek look (and same goes for black on black on black). Piles of white books beneath white chairs and atop the white cube in between produce a symmetrical vignette that feels über-modern and allows the artwork to pop.

The dichotomy of an all-white and an all-black book nook side by side is a sharp look. Inset shelves feature layered books, vases, and art for a refined aesthetic.

In Black and White

White and black don't necessarily draw the eye on their own, but when paired together or when used en masse, these colors have a powerful effect. Neutral book nooks have as much of an impact as colorful nooks, but with a wholly different vibe: They're simple and understated, yet polished.

Style an all-white or all-black alcove to let the surrounding décor shine. To spotlight a prized piece of art, for example, stick to a neutral palette of books. In this home, mostly white books, freed of their jackets, are turned so that their spines face the wall, and their white blocks of pages face outward. The only other décor on this table are a white stone statue and a bowl of white rocks. By adhering to a strictly white palette, you ensure there is nothing to draw the eye away from the showstopping artwork on the wall above. Try this same approach with black books on a piece of black furniture. Or mix it up with black books on a white table or white books on a black bookcase. The books immediately become part of the décor, a statement piece made neutral.

Neutrals aren't limited to black and white, of course. An all-gray nook would be very handsome. Alternatively, a black and navy or a cream and tan nook would work well too. Any of these monochrome and bichrome aesthetics is instantly chic. Keep them from looking dull by integrating lots of different textures and objects alongside your books.

OBERTO GILI
HOME SWEET HOME
Great Stud Farms of the World
A ROOM OF HER OWN
FORTUNY
NEW ARCHITECTURE OF THE AMERICAN SOUTH

GREAT HOLLYWOOD MOVIES
ABRADALE
EMBRYONIC LANDSCAPES
Leo Steinberg
OTHER CRITERIA
Chicago
THE ERROR OF MY WAYS
BEING AND TIME
HARPER & ROW
THE DISCO FILES 1973-78
New York's underground, week by week
d·a·p
SAN FRANCISCO IN THE SIXTIES
Igor Golomstock
TOTALITARIAN ART
COLLINS HARVILL
JOYCE TENNESON
INTIMACY
EMBRYONIC LANDSCAPES
ROBERT HUGHES
THE SHOCK OF THE NEW
Silver Masters of Mexico
Schiffer
vanabbemuseum
a companion to modern and contemporary art
LAPHAM'S QUARTERLY
COMMUNICATION
What Great Paintings Say
Volume 2
TASCHEN
modern architecture since 1900
CHAVE
Constantin Brancusi
Marcel Broodthaers
Walker Art Center
BETTINA RHEIMS
FEMALE TROUBLE
SCHIRMER ART BOOKS
SERRA
THE ADVENTURE OF DESIGN:
GAVINA

Opposites attract: Black and white make a bold statement and a perfect pair. Arrange black books on a white shelf or vice versa, or mix black and white books together for an arresting visual.

BOOKS BEYOND NOOKS

LITTLE FREE LIBRARIES

While this book is focused on creating nooks and styling books inside your home, there are many ways to reach beyond your own four walls and connect with your community by displaying and sharing books.

A beloved way to share a love of reading is by creating a mini free library just outside your home. Little free libraries are not too difficult to build yourself, or you can order one online. Bonus points if it matches your house! Once your mini library is set up, extend your newfound styling savvy to your doorstep: Paint it, add interior wallpaper, and fill it with books. Any kind of books will do, and a range of genres will capture a wider audience. If you have children's books to give away, be sure to include them—kids love discovering little free libraries in their neighborhood and helping themselves to a new book.

The point of a free library is, of course, that neighbors and passersby help themselves to a book and add a book of their own, so don't focus too much on the organization or arrangement of the books themselves. Check on your library every so often to ensure it's clean and well stocked—you don't want it empty of books but full of cobwebs!

Take inspiration from these examples of darling free libraries. Walk around your neighborhood and see if you can spot one or two.

Books make the world a better place, and recycling books is also sustainable. Installing a little free library in your front yard is a lovely, low-stakes way to contribute to your community.

Little Free Library

LittleFreeLibrary.org
AUSTIN
COLLEGES
CHANGE
LIVES
LOREN POPE

LittleFreeLibrary.org
Take a Book • Share a Book

LittleFreeLibrary

LittleFreeLibrary.org

LittleFreeLibrary

LittleFreeLibrary.org
Take a Book • Share a Book

CLASSIC LIBRARIES AROUND THE WORLD

Beyond little free libraries, real libraries offer myriad ways to connect with your community and interact with books beyond your own personal nooks. For centuries, libraries have existed as repositories of knowledge and ideas, resources for learning and inspiration, and centers of culture and community. Architects and designers have reveled in the creation of these beautiful buildings, from Thomas Burgh, the mastermind behind the hallowed halls of the Library of Trinity College in Ireland, to Joseph Hueber, who conceived of the cream and gold-trimmed Baroque-style Admont Abbey Library in Austria.

Classic libraries also offer plenty of interior design inspiration and ideas for creative storage for books. When designing your own book nook at home, look to the world's most impressive and historic libraries—or simply enjoy their beauty and add them to your travel bucket list! Here are a few to get you started.

1. Library of Trinity College, Dublin, Ireland (1592): Commissioned by Queen Elizabeth I, the Library of Trinity College houses more than six million works, including the Book of Kells, which dates back to the ninth century CE. If you're looking for truly classic library inspiration, check out the Long Room, a handsome two-storied, barrel-ceilinged hall lined with busts of iconic thinkers, writers, and philosophers. It feels like a setting from the world of Harry Potter.

2. Rampur Raza Library, Rampur, India (1774): Founded by Nawab Faizullah Khan—one of the Nawabs of Rampur, who were known to be forward-thinking—this architectural masterpiece, complete with stately minarets, is a trove of Indo-Islamic culture and heritage. It houses rare texts in Arabic, Persian, Pashto, Sanskrit, Urdu, Hindi, and Turkish languages. As any library should, this beautiful building encourages the pursuit of knowledge and makes you want to read. Make sure your book nook inspires those same feelings!

3. Admont Abbey Library, Admont, Austria (1776): Part of the Admont Abbey and Benedictine monastery, this white and gold library harkens back to the late Baroque period. Flooded with light, the hall features frescoed ceilings depicting seven scenes that illustrate the connection between science and religion. It's proof that classic libraries do not have to feature mahogany wood and dusty shelves—they can be light and airy too.

4. Royal Portuguese Cabinet of Reading, Rio de Janeiro, Brazil (1887): Three stories of intricately trimmed bookshelves store an invaluable collection of Portuguese literature. With three hundred and fifty thousand volumes—the largest collection outside of Portugal—not to mention the marble floors, gold and teal details, and a stained-glass ceiling, this majestic reading room by architect Rafael da Silva e Castro is a work of art.

5. The Stephen A. Schwarzman Building, New York, United States (1911): The main branch of the New York Public Library system, this Beaux Arts–style building in midtown Manhattan features a grand reading room and houses large collections of genealogical documents, rare books, maps, prints, and photographs. The exterior stairway is flanked by two marble lions, which have become trademarks of the library. Leo Astor and Leo Lenox, or Patience and Fortitude, make it so patrons can "read between the lions."

KHALED HOSSEINI AND THE MOUNTAINS ECHOED
UNFINISHED PALAZZO
IAN KERSHAW THE END
Historian
CLASSICAL LITERATURE
Alexander to Actium
AMERICA'S GREAT GAME
THE GOLDEN THREAD
THE WORLD OF LATE ANTIQUITY
LANARK
Forbidden American English
Max Ernst A Retrospective
ATHANASIUS KIRCHER'S Theatre of the World
THE NUDE
THE BLUE RIDER
The Library A WORLD HISTORY
C.G. JUNG A Biography in Books
CASINO ACROSS TIME
MONKSLAND ATHOS
BRUGES AND THE RENAISSANCE
DEMEURES HISTORIQUES
PAUSANIA HISTORIA
GREEK-ENGLISH LEXICON LIDDELL & SCOTT
POCOCKE TRAVELS
LES CHAMPS MAGNETIQUES
Albert Camus
Pablo Picasso
THE ELYSEE
CYPRUS
LA TERRE VUE DU CIEL
LE QUAI D'ORSAY
TO ΜΥΘΙΣΤΟΡΗΜΑ ΤΟΥ ΑΛΕΞΑΝΔΡΟΥ THE GREEK ALEXANDER ROMANCE
ΒΥΖΑΝΤΙΝΗ ΜΕΣΑΙΩΝΙΚΗ ΚΥΠΡΟΣ
ΠΟΡΤΡΕΤΑ ΤΟΥ ΦΑΓΙΟΥΜ
THE WASTE LAND T.S. ELIOT
PIRANESI UNBOUND
MY LIFE AS A WHORE
Fun Home ALISON BECHDEL
THE RULE OF FOUR
JOHN LE CARRÉ SILVERVIEW

PEN AMERICA'S Recommended Banned Books

"Books have a long history of being under attack in the United States. The scope of such censorship has expanded drastically in recent years. Books are disappearing from library shelves, being challenged in droves, and being decreed off-limits by school boards, legislators, and prison authorities. And everywhere, it is the books that have long fought for a place on the shelf that are being targeted: books by authors of color, by LGBTQIA+ authors, by women. Books about racism, sexuality, gender, and history. PEN America fights against the banning of books and the intolerance, exclusion, and censorship that undergird it."

—Kasey Meehan, Program Director of Freedom to Read

Kalynn Bayron, *Cinderella Is Dead*

Kacen Callender, *Hurricane Child*

Brandy Colbert, *The Only Black Girls in Town*

Mike Curato, *Flamer*

George M. Johnson, *All Boys Aren't Blue*

Maia Kobabe, *Gender Queer*

Kyle Lukoff and Kaylani Juanita, *When Aidan Became a Brother*

Bernard Malamud, *The Fixer*

Toni Morrison, *The Bluest Eye*

Molly Knox Ostertag, *The Girl from the Sea*

PEN AMERICA stands at the intersection of literature and human rights to protect free expression in the United States and worldwide. Their mission is to unite writers and their allies to celebrate creative expression and defend the liberties that make it possible. Join them in the fight. Sign up at www.pen.org.

Rembrandt's Eyes
JAMES ELLROY
Children's Literature
BIBLIO STYLE
CROSSROADS FRANZEN
SEVENTEEN
LITTLE EVE
KARL OVE KNAUSGAARD
NEIL GAIMAN
SURRENDER
MYSTERIES
New Zealand
Iceland
Chile
CELINE
THE RIVER PETER HELLER
REBEL CITY
LUSITANIA

MW01445328

A CATWALK AROUND THE WORLD

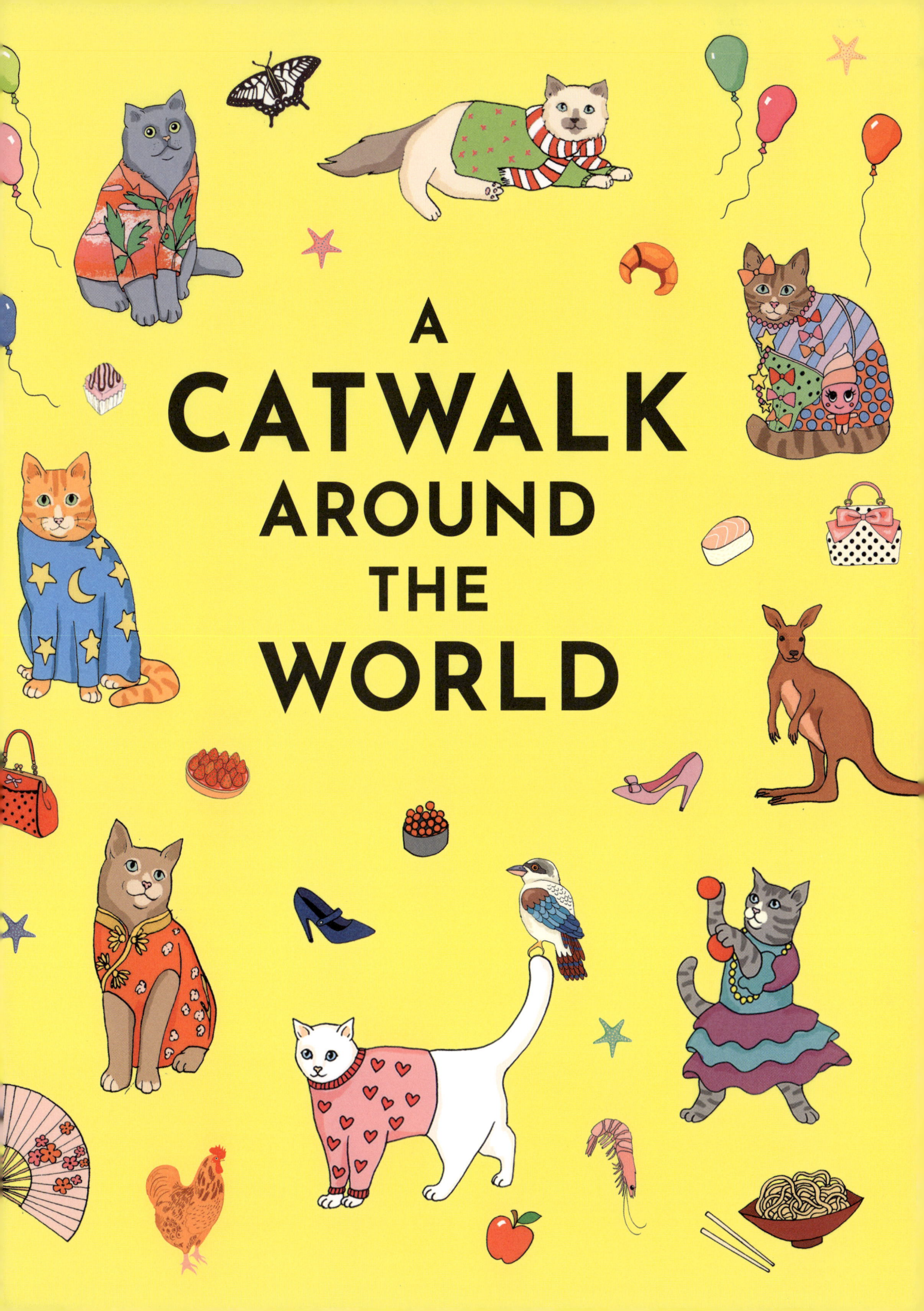

For my darling
daughter, Vivian. xxx
K. M.

LAURENCE KING

First published in Great Britain in 2025
by Laurence King

Text copyright © Hodder and Stoughton Ltd, 2025
Illustrations copyright © Karen Mabon, 2025

All rights reserved.
HB ISBN: 978-1-5102-3132-0

10 9 8 7 6 5 4 3 2 1

Printed in China

Laurence King
An imprint of
Hachette Children's Group
Part of Hodder and Stoughton
Carmelite House
50 Victoria Embankment
London EC4Y 0DZ

An Hachette UK Company
www.hachette.co.uk
www.hachettechildrens.co.uk
www.laurenceking.com

The authorised representative in the EEA is Hachette Ireland,
8 Castlecourt Centre, Dublin 15, D15 XTP3, Ireland (email: info@hbgi.ie)

KAREN MABON

A CATWALK AROUND THE WORLD

I'm **Vivian** the cat. Are you ready to explore the world with me?

LAURENCE KING

It's a glorious sunny day in the **Scottish Highlands**, home to **Vivian** the cat. Anticipation is in the air as the cats are getting ready for Burns' Night, but Vivian is excited for another reason—she's traveling the world, and you're invited to join her!

1. These cats are wearing bonnie wee clothes. Which of these traditional Scottish items of clothing can you spot the most of?

Kilt   Tweed   Tam o' Shanter cap

2. Your stomach is rumbling; you're hungry for Scottish cuisine. How many different Scottish delicacies can you spot?

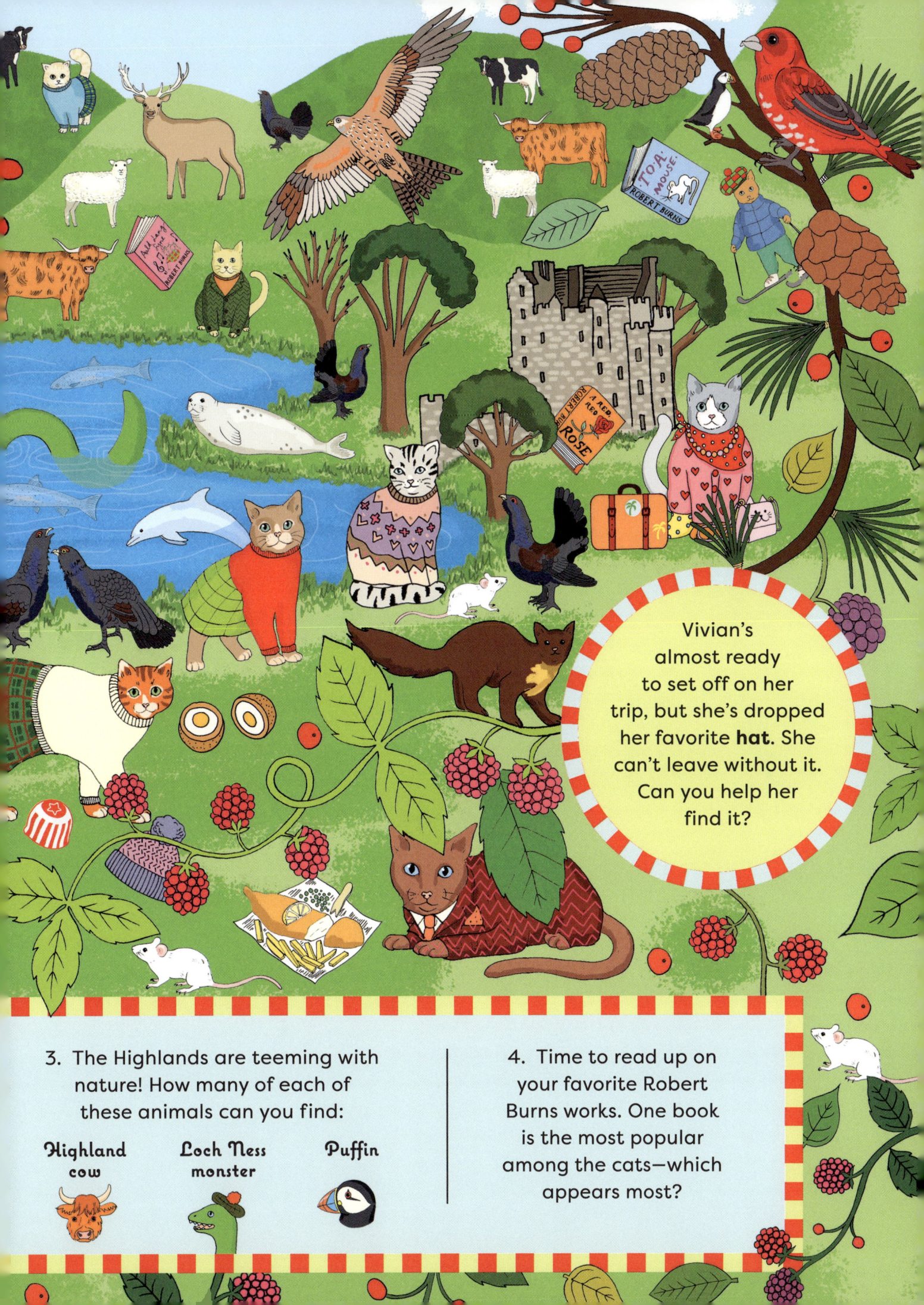

Vivian's almost ready to set off on her trip, but she's dropped her favorite **hat**. She can't leave without it. Can you help her find it?

3. The Highlands are teeming with nature! How many of each of these animals can you find:

Highland cow

Loch Ness monster

Puffin

4. Time to read up on your favorite Robert Burns works. One book is the most popular among the cats—which appears most?

The Scottish Highlands

With lots of wildlife, rolling hills and crystal-clear lakes, the Scottish Highlands are a nature lover's dream!

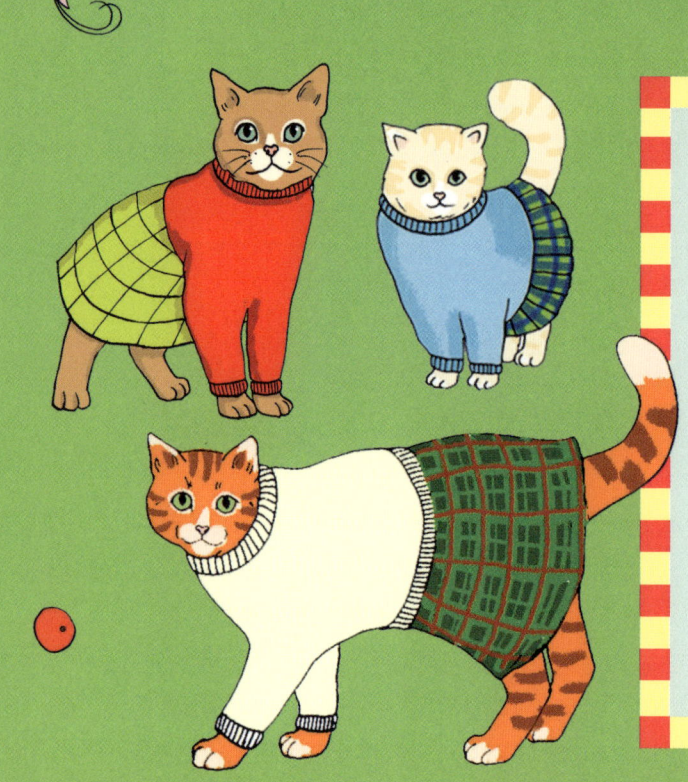

Kilts

A kilt is a wrap-around piece of clothing made of wool, with heavy pleats at the sides and back and traditionally a tartan pattern. It's not quite a skirt, though they look very similar! They're usually worn with a sporran, which is a small bag traditionally made from leather and fur.

Haggis

Haggis is a traditional Scottish dish made from a sheep's offal, which is the edible internal parts of an animal like the kidney and liver. It's mixed with suet (animal fat), oats and seasonings. Then it's boiled in a bag, traditionally one made from the animal's stomach! Sounds questionable, but if you serve it with neeps and tatties (turnips and potatoes) you're in for a truly tasty feast!

Loch Ness Monster

Also known as 'Nessie', the Loch Ness Monster is an enormous creature in Scottish folklore that is believed to live in the depths of Loch Ness. Do you think Nessie is real?

Burns' Night

Burns' Night is an evening of celebrations held in honor of the Scottish poet, Robert Burns. Held on or around January 25, Burns' birthday, the event can be celebrated by eating some haggis, reading Burns' poetry and laughing and dancing. It's a great night to party!

Paris

Salut and ciao! **Paris** and **Milan** Fashion Weeks are the most important dates in the calendar of any fashionista, so brush up on your fashion knowledge and spot some very stylish cats.

1. French and Italian designers have created some of the most iconic fashions in history. How many of these stylish accessories can you spot?

| Quilted bag | Pearl necklace | Chunky gold chains | Spiky shoes |

Milan

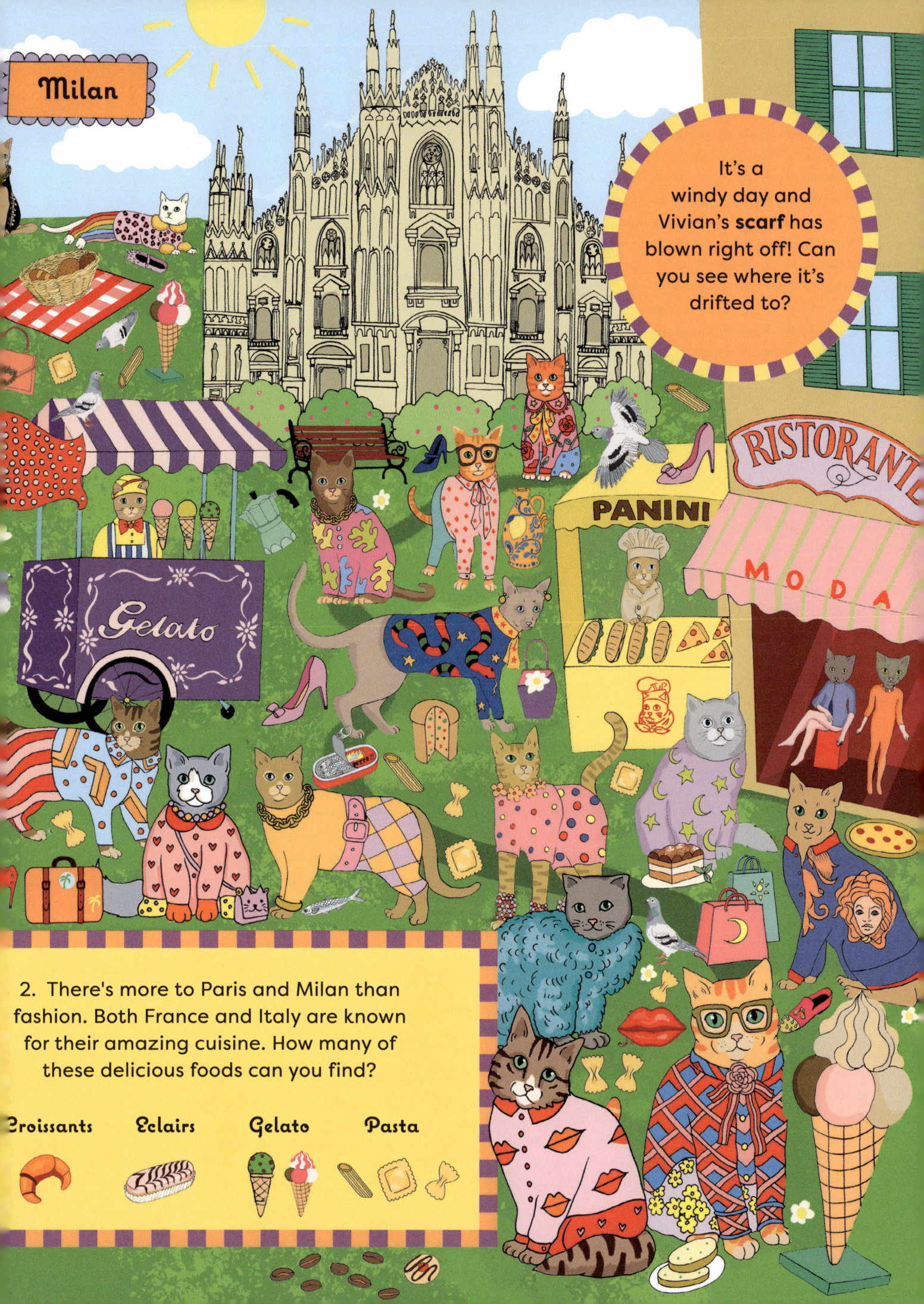

It's a windy day and Vivian's **scarf** has blown right off! Can you see where it's drifted to?

2. There's more to Paris and Milan than fashion. Both France and Italy are known for their amazing cuisine. How many of these delicious foods can you find?

Croissants   Eclairs   Gelato   Pasta

Paris and Milan

Paris and Milan are two of the Big Four fashion capitals of the world, along with London and New York City. No wonder all the cats there are so stylish!

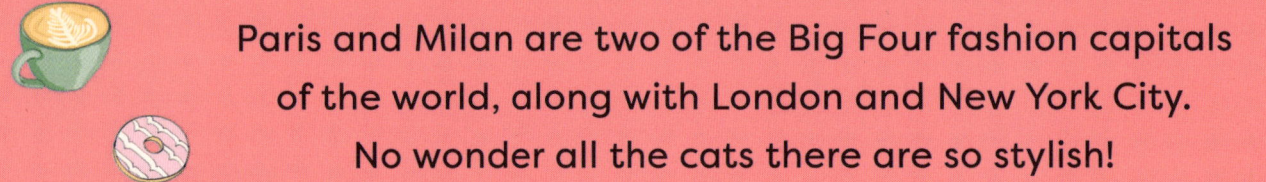

La Tour Eiffel

The Eiffel Tower is the iconic wrought-iron landmark of **Paris**. Standing at 984 feet, it's the tallest construction in Paris, as tall as an 81-storey building. It took twenty-two months to build.

Duomo di Milano

The Duomo in **Milan** is a huge cathedral famous for its impressive collection of 4,000 statues, gargoyles and other figures.

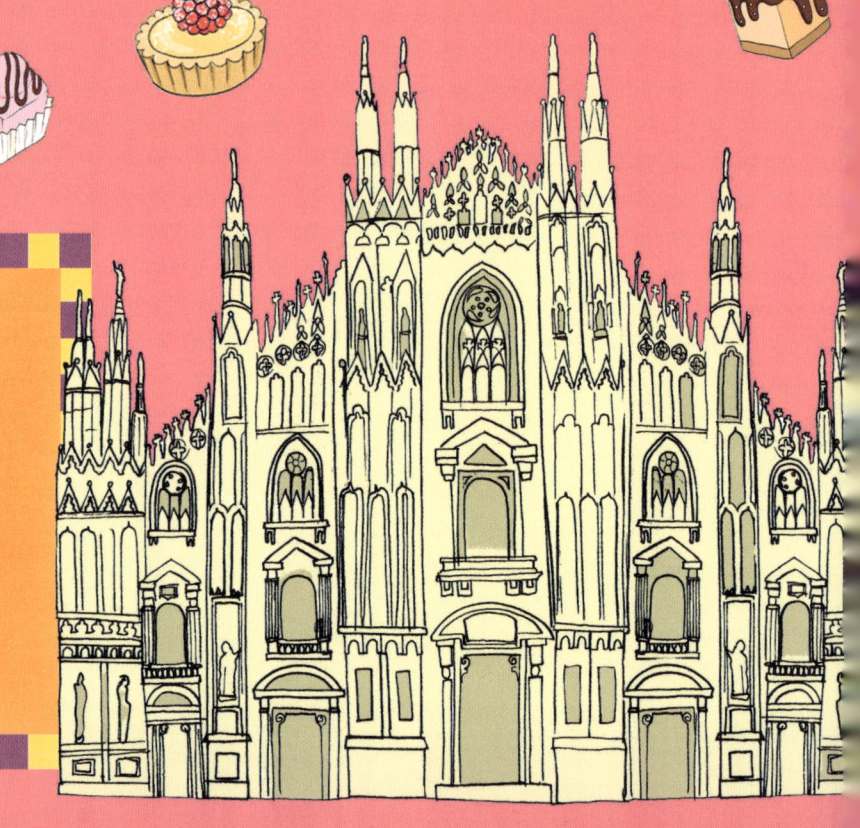

Designer Clothes

'Designer' clothes are fashionable, luxury clothing carrying the labels of well-known fashion designers such as Chanel, Dior and Versace. They're usually well-made and VERY expensive.

Fashion Week

Fashion week is a big fashion industry event that usually lasts—you guessed it!—a week, during which fashion designers, brands or 'houses' show their latest collections. These runway shows can effect future fashion trends. That means your favorite pair of shoes were possibly inspired by someone's runway design! A fashion 'house' isn't a building or house you live in. It's a company that designs and sells high-end fashion.

Panettone

Panettone is a sweet bread and fruitcake, originally from Milan. It is usually made and enjoyed for celebrations such as Christmas and New Year!

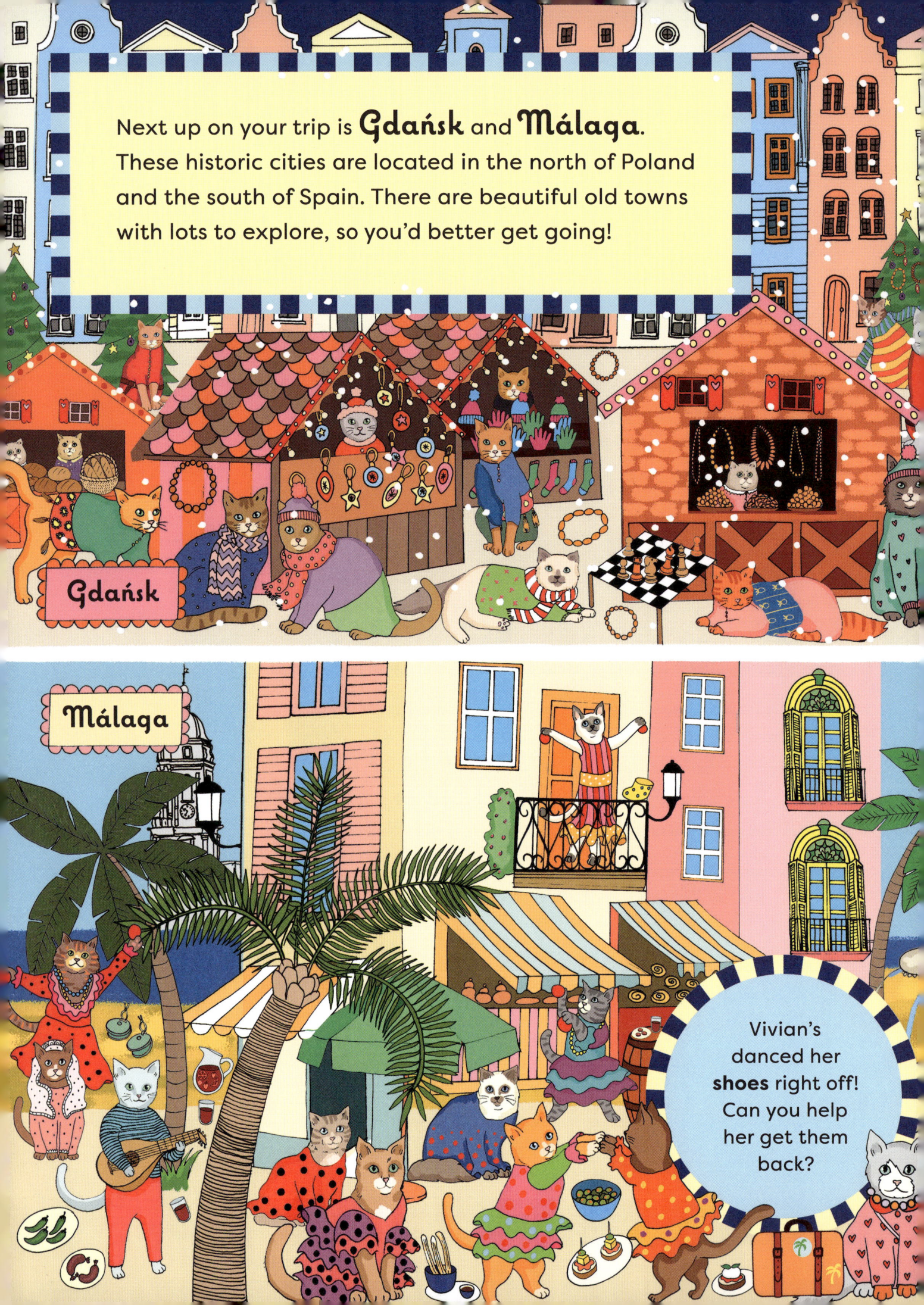

Next up on your trip is **Gdańsk** and **Málaga**. These historic cities are located in the north of Poland and the south of Spain. There are beautiful old towns with lots to explore, so you'd better get going!

Gdańsk

Málaga

Vivian's danced her **shoes** right off! Can you help her get them back?

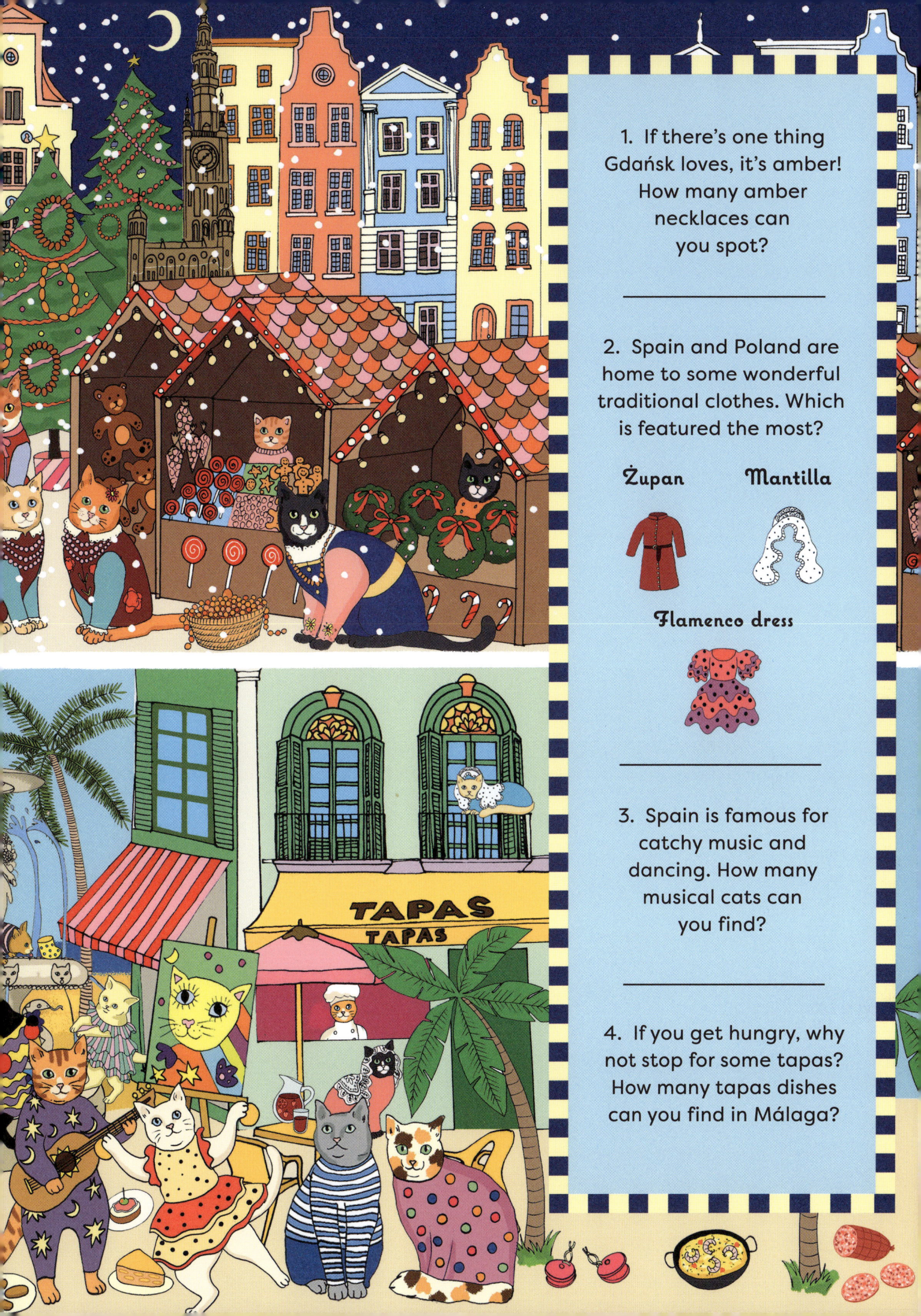

1. If there's one thing Gdańsk loves, it's amber! How many amber necklaces can you spot?

_____

2. Spain and Poland are home to some wonderful traditional clothes. Which is featured the most?

Żupan   Mantilla

Flamenco dress

_____

3. Spain is famous for catchy music and dancing. How many musical cats can you find?

_____

4. If you get hungry, why not stop for some tapas? How many tapas dishes can you find in Málaga?

Gdańsk and Málaga

Gdańsk and Málaga both boast rich heritages—Gdańsk is one of Poland's oldest cities, and Málaga is one of the oldest cities in the world!

Żupan

The żupan was a long robe worn by men, often made from silk and featuring decorative motifs.

Folk Costumes

Polish folk costumes are regional outfits that are rich in detail and are different from one area to another. For example, in the Łowicz region, women wear colourful striped skirts, white blouses, and floral scarves. Meanwhile, the Lachy Sądeckie folk costumes feature embroidered applications on jackets and trousers, and careful, delicate embroidery on corsets and shirts.

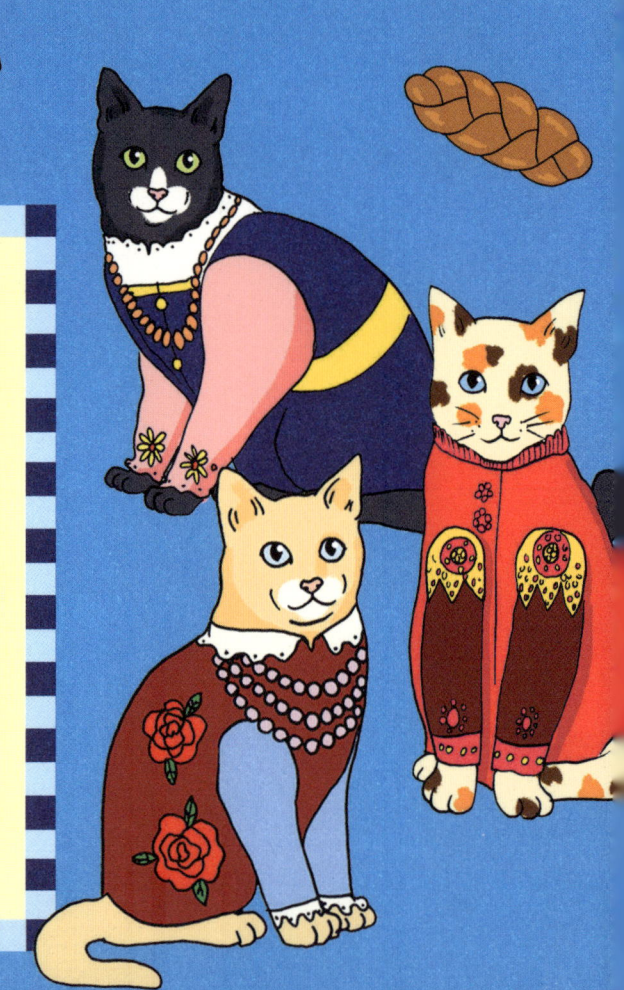

Amber

Gdańsk is the amber capital of the Baltic Sea, as most amber stones wash up along the beaches there. What is amber? It's fossilized (preserved) tree resin or gum, popular for its lovely orange colour.

Mantilla

This is a traditional Spanish lace or silk veil or shawl worn over the head and shoulders. Mantillas are often worn by women during Holy Week (the week leading up to Easter) and at weddings.

Flamenco

Flamenco is a style of entertainment with music and dance. Flamenco uses acoustic guitars, singing, hand claps, heel stamps, and castanets. It is danced in traditional Spanish costumes.

You're in **Amsterdam,** the Netherlands' capital. Boats are bobbing along the canal and everywhere you look people are riding colorful bicycles. Can you hear the wooden clogs clacking on the sidewalk?

1. The Netherlands is home to some of the most famous artists of all time. How many artist copycats can you find?

   _____

2. Amsterdam is in bloom—look at all those tulips! How many different colors are there?

   _____

3. If you've got a sweet tooth, you've come to the right place! Which of these treats can you spot the most of?

   - Stroopwafels
   - Apple tarts
   - Oliebollen (doughnuts)

Bloemen

Souvenirs

Snoep

Vivian took off her **gloves** to pick tulips, but now she can't find them! Where are they?

Amsterdam

Home to Europe's smallest house and the only floating flower market in the world, Amsterdam is the perfect destination for your catwalk around the world. And did you know there are more bikes in Amsterdam than people? (Well, cats, in this book.)

Clogs

Clogs are the iconic shoes of the Netherlands, and people have been wearing them for over 700 years. They're wooden slip-on shoes that are sturdy and—when stuffed with straw—nice and warm.

Tulips

Tulips were brought to the Netherlands in the sixteenth century and have been a symbol for the country ever since. The tulip is seen as a declaration of love, and every color has a deeper meaning. For example, yellow means happiness, and purple means royalty.

Stroopwafel

A stroopwafel is a thin, round waffle biscuit made from two layers of sweet baked dough held together by a caramel filling. You can lay a stroopwafel on top of a hot cup of tea or coffee to soften it before taking a bite into the oozing caramel. Delicious!

Vincent van Gogh

Vincent van Gogh (1853-1890) was born in Groot-Zundert in the Netherlands. Sadly, he suffered from mental health problems and used painting to help express his emotions. He only painted for about ten years, but in that short time he created more than 2,000 artworks, including the very famous *Sunflowers* and *The Starry Night*.

Rembrandt

Rembrandt Harmenszoon van Rijn (1609-1669) was born in Leiden in the Netherlands and is considered the most important painter in Dutch history. He produced an estimated 600 paintings, including *The Anatomy Lesson*, and 1,400 drawings.

You've arrived at the longest human-made structure in the world, **The Great Wall of China.** It's so long that it would take you seventeen months to walk across it! It's China's most famous landmark, so there are tourists everywhere.

There are twelve animals in the Chinese Zodiac. Can you find them all?

- Rat
- Ox
- Tiger
- Rabbit
- Dragon
- Snake
- Horse
- Ram
- Monkey
- Rooster
- Dog
- Pig

Vivian's **bag** slipped right off her shoulder when she was at one of the wall's viewpoints! Where's it gone?

1. All this traveling has left you feeling a little under the weather. Time to recuperate with some Chinese medicine and exercise. How many cats can you see Chinese cupping and practising tai chi?

2. Once again, your stomach's rumbling! How many different types of mouth-watering Chinese food can you spot?

The Great Wall of China

The Great Wall of China is a impressive 69,540 feet long and took over 2,000 years to build. Construction of the wall started in 220 BCE and was built for defensive purposes, which is why it's so huge. You can't see it from space, though—that's just a rumor! And the Great Wall is not the only icon of China's rich heritage.

Chèuhngsāam

The chèuhngsāam is a close-fitting silk dress with a high circular collar, side slits, and an asymmetrical opening at the front, traditionally secured with knotted buttons and loops. There are different styles of chèuhngsāam in Beijing, Shanghai, and Hong Kong, with many differences in the decorations, colors, materials, and designs.

Tángzhuāng (Tang Suit)

A Tángzhuāng is a traditional Chinese jacket usually made from silk, brocade, or cotton. Originally designed for men, it is now worn by both men and women on special occasions, such as at weddings or at Lunar New Year celebrations.

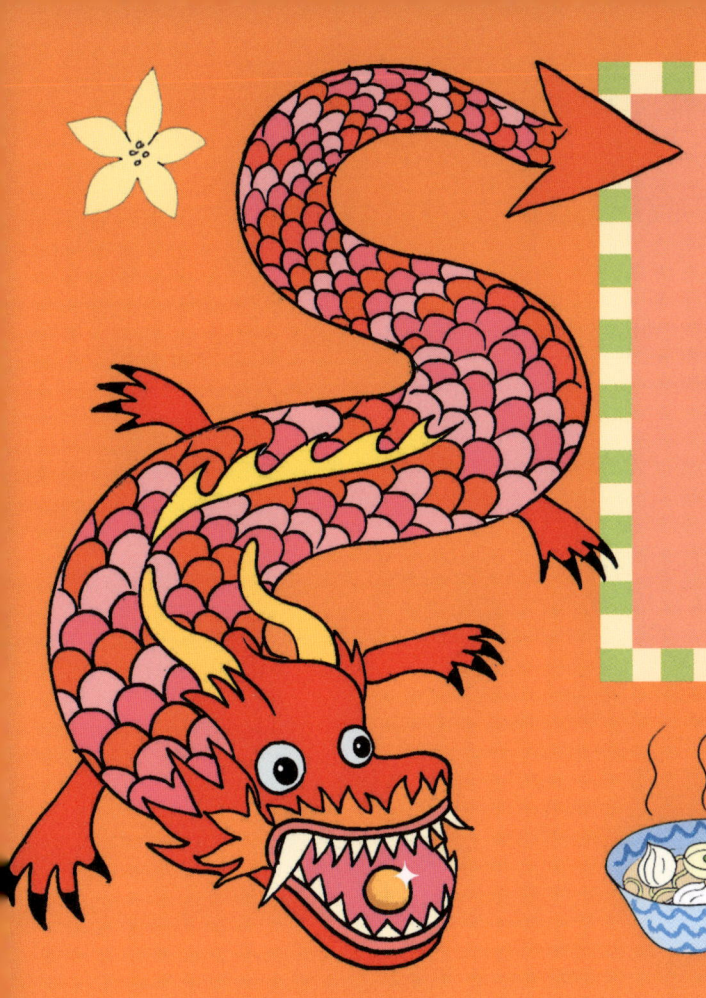

Chinese Zodiac

Every year represents one of the twelve individual animals of the Chinese Zodiac, which according to legend, raced each other. For example, the year 2000 was the Year of the Dragon. Do you know which animal year were you born on?

Tai chi

Chinese Medicine and Martial Arts

Traditional Chinese medicine has been used for thousands of years and is based on a philosophy of balance with nature.

Chinese cupping is a treatment using heating cups on the skin to increase blood flow to the affected area.

Tai Chi was first developed as a martial art in China, but it is now a popular form of exercise. It involves a series of slow gentle movements performed with controlled breathing. It is very relaxing!

Cupping

Kon'nichiwa (hello), and welcome to **Tokyo**. With both traditional shrines and high-tech robots, Japan's capital is the perfect blend of traditional and modern. Take it all in!

Vivian's bought a flower chain in an outdoor market, but she's dropped her old **necklace**. Better find it before you have to say sayōnara (goodbye)!

1. Japan has many beautiful traditional clothes and eye-catching styles to offer! Which is featured the most?

Kimono

Harajuku

_____

2. There is some truly beautiful nature to spot in Japan, even in a busy metropolis like Tokyo! How many different types of flowers can you spot?

_____

3. Grab your chopsticks and a bottle of soy sauce—it's lunchtime! Can you find the following ingredients to make a bowl of ramen for yourself and a friend?

2 x nests of noodles

2 x soy sauce

4 x eggs

4 x chopsticks

Tokyo

Tokyo is a fast-paced city famous for incredible fashion, anime, electronics, and vending machines that sell everything from hamburgers to umbrellas! It's home to one of the busiest pedestrian crossings in the world, Shibuya Crossing, which sees a huge average of 300,000 crossers every day.

Kimono

Kimonos have been worn for over a thousand years and are the national dress of Japan. They have square sleeves and a rectangular body and are traditionally worn with a broad sash called an obi and accessories such as zōri sandals and tabi socks.

Yukata

A yukata is another type of traditional robe, similar to the kimono. 'Yukata' literally means 'bathing cloth'—it was traditionally worn after a dip in a communal bath or an onsen (hot spring).

Harajuku Street Style

As well as being one-of-a-kind, colorful, and fun, Harajuku fashion celebrates community and freedom of expression.

Mochi

Mochi is a Japanese dessert made of sweet glutinous (sticky) rice flour. Mochi dough is often tinted with matcha (green tea powder) or other food colorings and wrapped around a sweet center. This delicious bite-sized dessert has a chewy, smooth, and elastic texture.

Cherry Blossom

The blossom of the cherry tree is known as sakura in Japanese. It symbolizes the return of spring, as well as renewal and hope. The perfect pink petals only bloom for about a week, so see them while you can!

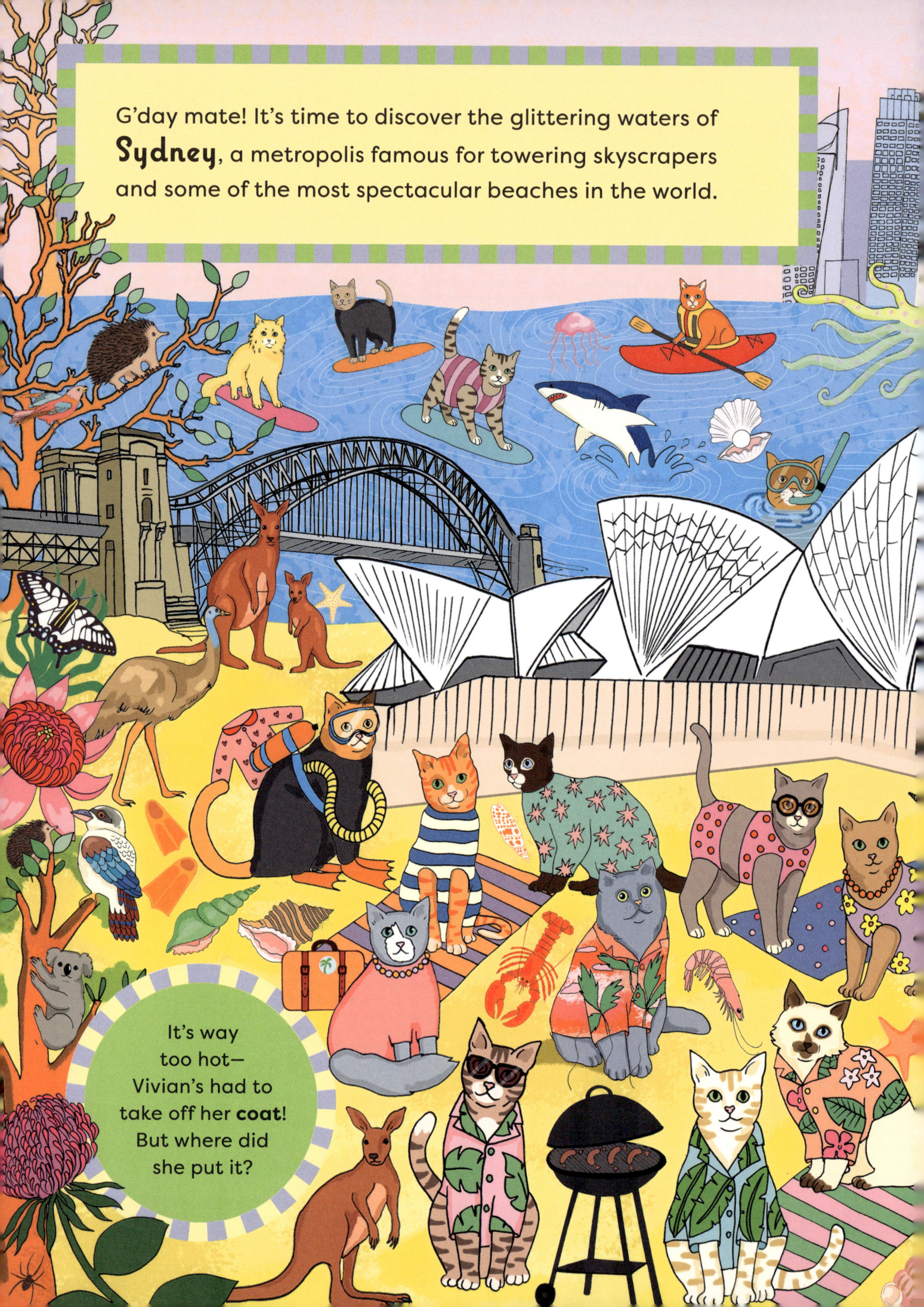

G'day mate! It's time to discover the glittering waters of **Sydney**, a metropolis famous for towering skyscrapers and some of the most spectacular beaches in the world.

It's way too hot—Vivian's had to take off her **coat**! But where did she put it?

1. With the harbor and over a hundred beaches, there are many water sports on offer in Sydney. Which different water sports can you spot?

_____

2. Australia is full of unique animals. How many of each of these animals can you find?

Koala   **Kangaroo**   **Echidna**

_____

3. As well as animals, Australia is home to lots of special trees. Which type of tree has the most animals in its branches?

Eucalyptus   **Waratah**

Gum Tree

Sydney

Sydney officially became a city in 1842. Despite what a lot of people think, Sydney's not the capital city of Australia—that would be Canberra. With the Blue Mountains in the distance, and its incredible beaches, it's no surprise that Sydney is a hugely popular tourist spot.

The Sydney Opera House

The Sydney Opera House is one of the world's most famous buildings and Australia's most recognisable human-made landmark. It was opened by Queen Elizabeth II in 1973 and is so big that about 15,500 light bulbs must be changed there every year. Just imagine the electricity bill!

Harbour Bridge

The Sydney Harbour Bridge is tallest steel arch bridge in the world, standing at 493 feet from top to water level. It's nicknamed "the coat hanger" because of its arch-based design, but you'd have a hard time hanging your clothes on something so tall.

Australian Animals

Most of Australia's animals are endemic, which means they are found nowhere else in the world. Platypuses, wombats, emus, and Tasmanian devils are some of the many animals that you can only find in Australia. Did you find the other endemic animals on the previous spread?

Wombat

Platypus

Tasmanian devil

Emu

Australian Plants

There are many endemic plants in Australia too. The red-pink gum tree is a favourite of koalas and the furry kangaroo paw is named for its velvety flowers that look like—you guessed it!—kangaroo paws.

Gum tree

Kangaroo paw

Welcome to the city that never sleeps—**New York**—the perfect destination to end your catwalk around the world! Your senses are in overdrive—you can smell the pizza, hear the busy traffic, and see so many dazzling city lights. Where to begin?

1. Theatre enthusiasts love New York for one reason—Broadway! How many wonderful Broadway cat spin-off shows can you spot?

2. New York never sleeps so it's important to keep your energy up. Let's go for a pizza! How many slices of pizza can you spot in this scene?

3. It's been a great trip, but it's time to head home. Hail down the yellow cab without a passenger. Hey—**taxi!**

You've finally caught up with Vivian, and she's wearing a whole new outfit! All she needs now is her **suitcase**. Can you help her find it?

New York

With lots of culture and entertainment to offer, and home to approximately 8.5 million people, the Big Apple is one of the most exciting cities to visit in the USA—and the world!

Broadway

The best New York shows, from up-and-coming plays to big and bold musicals, take place in the over forty professional theatres in the Broadway district. Broadway itself has some longstanding superstitions, from breaking a leg (which actually means good luck), to not whistling in a theatre, to the use of a ghost light to ward off spirits. Spooky!

The Empire State Building

Once the tallest building in the world, the Empire State Building was built in 1931. Its art deco design is thought to have been based on the humble pencil, and with up to 3,400 workers teaming up on its construction every day, it only took twenty months to complete.

The Statue of Liberty

'Lady Liberty' was a present from France to the American people as a monument to American freedom. The statue, which stands at 150 feet, sways in the wind, so be careful climbing her on a blustery day!

Film and TV

As it's such a dynamic, interesting city, with a huge variety of people, landmarks, and neighborhoods, New York is the setting of many beloved movies and TV shows. So if the city looks familiar to you, that might be why!

New York Cabs

An entrepreneur, Harry N. Allen, started the New York Taxicab Company in 1907 to compete with very high fares for the horse-drawn carriages on the streets of New York. He imported sixty-five cars from France and painted them a distinguishable yellow.

Answers

Scotland
1. Kilts — five cats are wearing them. Tweed: three cats; Tam o' Shanter cap: two cats.
2. Eight — shortbread; porridge; Empire biscuit; fish and chips; cranachan; haggis, neeps and tatties; tea cake, scotch egg.
3. Three highland cows, one Loch Ness monster, three puffins.
4. *To a Mouse* — four copies. *A Red, Red Rose*: three copies; *Auld Lang Syne*: two copies.

Paris and Milan
1. Quilted bags: four; Pearl necklaces: seven; Chunky gold chains: three; Spiky shoes: two.
2. Croissants: four; eclairs: four; gelato: five; pasta: eleven.

Gdańsk and Málaga
1. Eighteen amber necklaces.
2. Flamenco Dresses — eight cats are wearing them. Żupan: two cats; mantilla: three cats.
3. Seven musical cats.
4. Thirteen dishes — churros, olives, tortilla, cured ham, padrón peppers, croquettes, paella, prawn tapa, Spanish crostini, cheese tapa, chorizo, and cured ham tapa.

Amsterdam
1. Three copycat artists — Rembrandt, van Gogh and Vermeer.
2. Six colours of tulips — red, orange, yellow, pink, purple and white.
3. Stroopwafel — there are fourteen. Apple tarts: four; oliebollen: thirteen.

China
1. Tai Chi: six cats; cupping: five cats.
2. Seven — congee, chuan meat skewer, sticky rice, spring rolls, wontons, chow mein, and wonton soup.

Tokyo
1. Kimono — ten cats are wearing them. Harajuku: 5 cats.
2. Five types of flower — cherry blossom, golden-rayed lily, lotus flower, violets and camellia.

Sydney
1. Canoeing; surfing; snorkeling; scuba diving
2. Koala: four; kangaroo: four; echidna: five
3. Waratah has the most — six. Gum tree: five; eucalyptus: three.

New York
1. There are seven — *Wicked, Cats, Frozen, The Sound of Music, The Lion King, The Phantom of the Opera* and *Elvis: The Musical*.
2. Eight slices of pizza.